Andrew Clemson is a Chartered Trade Mark Attorney and partner at Cleveland Scott York. He has over 19 years of experience in trade mark law and practice.

He works with clients in the UK, Europe and globally on the full range of trade mark clearance, filing and prosecution work as well as in the contentious areas of infringements, oppositions and domain name disputes.

Andrew regularly presents lectures and seminars on domain name disputes and trade mark law.

A Practical Guide to the Law of Domain Names and Cybersquatting

Second Edition

A Practical Guide to the Law of Domain Names and Cybersquatting

Second Edition

Andrew Clemson
BSc, LLM, MCITMA
Chartered Trade Mark Attorney
Partner, Cleveland Scott York LLP

Law Brief Publishing

Published 2026 by Law Brief Publishing, an imprint of Law Brief Publishing Ltd
30 The Parks
Minehead
Somerset
TA24 8BT

www.lawbriefpublishing.com

Paperback: 978-1-918241-08-2

With thanks to Bex, Matthew and James
for all the tea, hugs and support that
have made this book possible.

PREFACE

The World Intellectual Property Organization ("WIPO") reported in January 2025 that it handled 6,168 cybersquatting cases in 2024. This represents a 134% increase over the last decade. The figures for 2025 are set to be even higher.

Retail, banking, pharmaceuticals and IT are commonly targeted sectors – but any business with an online presence is at risk from cybersquatting or cybercriminal activity.

This book is intended as a practical guide for in-house and private practice legal professionals who already have some familiarity with trade mark law, domain names and the various domain name dispute mechanisms.

It provides practical advice on how to avoid domain name disputes arising in the first instance and best practice for taking action if disputes do arise.

The law surrounding domain name disputes is complex, international and constantly changing. It is far beyond the scope of this book to tackle all areas within this broad remit.

Instead, the author seeks to provide guidance from a neutral standpoint, for both complainants and respondents, focussing on the Uniform Domain Name Dispute Resolution Policy ("UDRP") for generic top level domains, the Nominet Dispute Resolution Service for the *.uk* country code top level domain and the EUR*id* ADR for the *.eu* country code top level domain.

The UDRP is discussed in most detail and current trends in panellists' decisions are highlighted. The Nominet Dispute Resolution Service and the EUR*id* ADR are reviewed in a comparative fashion.

The various country code top level domain dispute mechanisms (other than *.uk* and *.eu*) are not covered and neither are any other areas of Internet law that might be tangentially related to domain names.

This second edition of the book states the law as at 30 September 2025.

Andrew Clemson
September 2025

CONTENTS

PART A

INTRODUCTION AND BACKGROUND

CHAPTER ONE

BACKGROUND AND BASICS

The IT world is very fond of its technical language and jargon. The terminology around domain names is no exception.

1.1 Definitions

It is helpful at the outset to provide definitions and explanations of some common terms that are used throughout this book.

TLD	Top Level Domain. The letters found at the end of a domain name address, such as *.com*, *.uk*, or *.london*
ccTLD	Country Code TLD. Any TLD that represents a specific country or territory, such as *.uk*, *.eu* or *.de*
gTLD	One of the 22 original legacy generic Top Level Domains, namely *.aero*, *.asia*, *.biz*, *.cat*, *.com*, *.coop*, *.edu*, *.gov*, *.info*, *.int*, *.jobs*, *.mil*, *.mobi*, *.museum*, *.name*, *.net*, *.org*, *.post*, *.pro*, *.tel*, *.travel* and *.xxx*
New gTLD	A gTLD other than the 22 legacy gTLDs.
SLD	Second level domain/2nd level domain. The letters immediately preceding the TLD. For example, the "*.co*" in *google.co.uk* and "google" in *google.com* are both SLDs.
Domain name	The combination of the SLD and the TLD – and including any letter string at the third level, where present. For example, "*google.com*" and "*google.co.uk*". (Used interchangeably with "domain")

ASCII	American Standard Code for Information Interchange.
IDN	Internationalized Domain Names.
ICANN	Internet Corporation for Assigned Names and Numbers.
DNS	The Domain Name System.
Registrar	A company whose business is the allocation of domain names to individuals or companies.
Registrant	The individual or company that contracts with a Registrar to register a domain name.
Registry	The entity which controls all of the domain names within a TLD.
Nominet	The Registry which controls the *.uk*, *.wales* and *.cymru* ccTLDs.
EUR*id*	The Registry which controls the *.eu*, *.ею* and *.ευ* ccTLDs.
Root zone	The central authoritative database for the DNS.
UDRP	The Uniform Domain-Name Dispute-Resolution Policy.
URS	The Uniform Rapid Suspension System.
DRS	The Dispute Resolution Service. Nominet's domain name dispute mechanism for the *.uk* ccTLD

EUR*id* ADR	The domain name dispute mechanism for the *.eu*, *.ею* and *.ευ* ccTLDs.
WIPO	World Intellectual Property Organization
ADNDRC	The Asian Domain Name Dispute Resolution Centre.
FORUM	The Forum (formerly The National Arbitration Forum).
TMCH	The Trademark Clearing House.
IPEC	The Intellectual Property Enterprise Court.

1.2 Why are domain names important?

Domain names are the Internet's global telephone directory matching up hard-to-remember strings of numbers with easy-to-remember words. They have been essential for finding and identifying computers since the earliest days of the Internet.

At the end of the first quarter of 2025 there were:[1]

- 368.4 million domain name registrations across all TLDs
- 142.9 million domain name registrations across all ccTLDs
- 169.8 million domain name registrations in the *.com* and *.net* gTLDs
- 37.8 million domain name registrations across all New gTLDs

1 The Verisign Domain Name Industry Brief, Q1 2025

As of 31 March 2025, there were 316 ccTLD extensions the top ten[2] of which account for 58.3 % of all ccTLD registrations.

A domain name and its associated website is commonly a brand owner's most direct means of contact with its customers. On a technical level, the domain name also supports critical functions such as email, websites and e-commerce platforms.

Internet users rely on the domain name to signpost the brand owner's legitimate website and email. When this is tampered with the effects can be immediate and severe.

We are all aware these days of the risks associated with hacking and scams on-line. Hacks which target the ownership of and control over domain names themselves can be extremely damaging. In July 2024, the migration of domain names from Google Domains over to Squarespace left a vulnerability which allowed hackers to take control of hundreds of cryptocurrency domains controlling access to billions of dollars of assets. The traffic to these websites was then diverted[3] after hackers changed the domains' DNS settings. Internet users were taken to potentially malicious websites where their credentials and other data could have been harvested. There are many other similar examples.

1.3 Why are domain name dispute mechanisms important?

In the early days of the Internet, some companies were slow to realise how important it was going to be and how valuable it would be to them to own the domain name corresponding to their brand.

There were systems in place for preventing cybersquatting, but they were crude and ineffective and third parties were easily able to buy up domain names consisting of famous brands in the hope of selling them on at a

2. *cn*; . *.de*; *.uk*; *.ru*; *.nl*; *.br*; .au; .fr; .in; *.eu*

3 https://www.securityweek.com/hackers-exploit-flaw-in-squarespace-migration-to-hijack-domains/

profit. Famously, the mcdonalds.com domain name was first registered in 1994 by a journalist as part of a story highlighting the problem of cybersquatting.[4]

ICANN was concerned that the lack of a guaranteed link between the owner of the domain name and the trade mark shown in the domain name was threatening the very legitimacy of the DNS. Accordingly, they tasked WIPO to come up with a mechanism whereby brand owners could take back ownership of any domains that had been registered in bad faith and thus restore public confidence in the DNS. In 1999, following a global consultation process, ICANN launched the Uniform Domain-Name Dispute-Resolution Policy.

The domain name dispute mechanisms promote trust and brand integrity on the Internet and minimise the burden on national courts. They also provide a safe harbour for ICANN, the registries and the registrars who might otherwise get dragged into court proceedings whenever a domain is registered in bad faith.

Ultimately, without effective domain name dispute mechanisms in place the DNS would be lawless and the Internet as we know it today would cease to function.

4 https://www.wired.com/1994/10/mcdonalds/

CHAPTER TWO

THE EFFECT OF GDPR

In the good old days it was very easy to find out the owner of a domain name. Every registrar was obliged to collect registrant contact details when selling a domain name and these details were all collected into the global WhoIs database.

Anyone could then simply type the domain name into the database to return the details of the person or business which had registered it. It was also possible to conduct an historic WhoIs search to check for previous owners of the domain and a reverse WhoIs search to obtain a listing of all domains owned by a particular registrant. This information was invaluable to the security services, law enforcement and brand owners.

In recent years, the growth of privacy and proxy services and the General Data Protection Regulation[5] ("GDPR") have caused a WhoIs blackout. It is now much more difficult to ascertain the true owner of a domain name.

2.1 GDPR vs RDAP WhoIs

It is fair to say that ICANN has made a bit of a mess of its GDPR compliance.

Despite knowing for years that the law was coming and being warned by the EU Commission that much of the publicly available WhoIs data would fall foul of it, it left the implementation of its response to the 11th hour.

5 General Data Protection Regulation 2016/679; https://eur-lex.europa.eu/eli/reg/2016/679/oj

Even then the response was to implement the Temporary Specification for gTLD Registration Data (the "Temporary Specification") to amend the process of collecting and publishing WhoIs data. The registries and registrars were only informed of the final detail of the Temporary Specification on 17 May 2018, just one week before the GDPR came into force.

The Temporary Specification was rushed through under ICANN's Temporary Policy mechanism, representing the first time that this mechanism had ever been used. It set out the rules[6] for the collection and publication of WhoIs data in a post-GDPR world. The aim being to ensure that registries and registrars were able to fulfil their contractual requirements to ICANN and be GDPR compliant during the transition to a permanent replacement.

As the name suggests, the Temporary Specification was temporary and it expired on 26 August 2019. ICANN carried out an Expedited Policy Development Process to finalise the details of its permanent replacement WhoIs policy – the Registration Data Access Protocol (RDAP).

The RDAP became the definitive source for delivering registration information on 28 January 2025. It is primarily a back-office upgrade and allows users to access the same redacted domain name registration data that was available under the Temporary Specification. However, the way that the data is collected and accessed has been standardised making the system more robust and allowing certain organisations (e.g. law enforcement) to have more open access.

ICANN has created a free-to-use RDAP Web Client[7] which third parties can use to access domain name registration data.

6 https://www.icann.org/resources/pages/gtld-registration-data-specs-en

7 https://lookup.icann.org/en

The disclosure of redacted registration data is possible using ICANN's new Registration Data Request Service[8] (RDRS) portal or by contacting the concerned registrar directly. The request must indicate the specific data for which disclosure is requested, the country in which that data will be used and the specific reason why the data is needed.

Nominet, the guardian of the *.uk* namespace, has a Data Release Request Form[9] available for download on its website. A registrant's personal data will be released upon the request of law enforcement or trade mark holders or their representatives who are preparing to file a DRS complaint or other enforcement action.

Nominet will, unless prohibited by law or likely to damage the rights of others, inform the registrant that a disclosure has been made, which information has been disclosed and to whom it has been sent. Brand owners should bear in mind, therefore, that use of the Data Release Request Form might tip off an infringer that enforcement action is potentially on the horizon.

EUR*id* has a similar Personal Data Disclosure Form[10] for domains in the *.eu*, *.ею* and *.ευ* ccTLDs. It does not notify the registrant when data has been released.

---

8 https://rdrs.icann.org/; https://www.icann.org/en/system/files/files/rdrs-user-guide-requestors-21jan25-en.pdf. An ICANN on-line account is required.

9 https://www.nominet.uk/privacy-notice/releasing-your-personal-data-to-third-parties/; https://www.nominet.uk/wp-content/uploads/2025/03/DataReleaseForm.pdf

10 https://cdn.eurid.eu/assets/request_form_for_registration_data_disclosure_p-21.pdf

2.2 GDPR vs UDRP and URS

UDRP and URS providers took the implementation of GDPR in their stride. From their perspective, the challenges it created were no different to those caused by the use of privacy/proxy services which they were already quite used to handling.

Providers will accept "Name Redacted" as the respondent initially listed in a complaint. Once the UDRP/URS action is underway, registrars should have no difficulty in handing over the full registrant details to the provider on the basis that they meet Article 6(1)(f) "legitimate purposes" and Article 6(1)(b) "performance of a contract" criteria of the GDPR. The complainant can then update the details of the complaint should it choose to do so.

The procedures and considerations surrounding consolidation of UDRP proceedings will remain the same but, in the absence of registrant contact information, panels may have to rely on other indications that the relevant domains are in common control.[11]

11 WIPO UDRP Overview 3.0, paragraph 4.11.2

PART B

AVOIDING DISPUTES

CHAPTER THREE

STANDARD STEPS TO TAKE

It is true in law, as indeed it is in life in general many would say, that the best type of dispute is the one that never happens. Domain name law is certainly an area where some prior thought and planning can avoid disputes arising and thus save a great deal of time and effort down the line.

Therefore, before turning to the various different strategies and procedures for resolving disputes, it is appropriate to consider the steps that one might take to avoid a dispute arising in the first instance.

These steps can be further divided down into those to be taken when protecting an existing portfolio and those necessary when protecting a product or venture for the first time.

3.1 What and where to register?

Having a clear understanding of exactly which domain names should be registered is critical both to the utility of the portfolio and to avoiding disputes. This requires consideration of exactly what to register (i.e. the second level domain letter string) and where to register it (i.e. in which TLDs).

The ideal scenario would be for a rights owner to identify the boundaries of which domains it might want and then register every such domain at the outset. It could then rest secure in the knowledge that no action would ever need to be brought against a cybersquatter as ownership of all other domains has already been considered been deemed to be unnecessary. This would allow resources to be allocated to more serious domain name disputes relating to counterfeiting, spoofing and similar issues. Of course, in practice, this is not likely to be feasible so brand owners should adopt a graduated approach to domain registration making sure that as many key domains as possible are protected within the portfolio.

The obvious starting point when creating an effective domain name portfolio is to produce a detailed schedule of all of the domains that have already been registered. This will not only highlight any gaps that need to be filled but will also provide an opportunity to check that all of the registrant details for each registration are correct and that the renewal deadline has been logged.

Another key early step is to cross reference the domain name portfolio schedule with the existing portfolio of trade marks. Any brands which are considered sufficiently business-critical to be the subject of trade mark registrations should certainly be reflected in the domain name portfolio.

Ultimately, the decision about which domains to register will depend upon the nature of the business in question and how the relevant decision makers perceive the potential risks of *not* registering those domains.

Brand owners should avoid indiscriminate registration as this will result in a very large portfolio that has no real business benefit. Instead, it is preferable have a targeted portfolio with a clear business rationale behind which domain names are owned and why.

Regarding what second level domains to register, brand owners should consider the following points:

- What am I trying to achieve with the portfolio?

- How do customers find the business / product?

- What will the domain be used for? Will it point to its own website? Will it re-direct to a website at a different domain? Will it be purely defensive?

- Reflect the house mark / product name / company name / slogan / tag line / short-term project name with domain name registrations?

- Is the business predominantly online based? That is to say, is the business related to goods for which there is an e-commerce website or is the business advisory in nature and largely conducted over email?

- Are internationalised domains or translations/transliterations into local languages likely to be necessary?

- Should any domain names be registered defensively? (this is discussed in more detail at paragraph 3.9 below)

- Would it be worthwhile to register a New gTLD? (this is discussed in more detail at paragraph 3.10 below)

Once a strategy has been reached about which second level domains should be protected it falls to consider where they should be protected. Again, an indiscriminate approach will just result in an unnecessarily large and costly portfolio so it is worth spending some time deciding which TLDs will be relevant.

Brand owners should consider the following points:

- The key original gTLDs with open registration requirements will nearly always need to be covered (e.g. *.com*; *.org*; *.net*)

- Identify any relevant New gTLDs. That is to say that if the business revolves around the provision of legal services in London, then registration in the *.law* and *.london* New gTLD registries might be appropriate. Registration in the *.ninja* registry is perhaps less likely to be required. This is discussed in more detail in Chapter 4

- In respect of ccTLDs, the home market / key sales markets / manufacturing markets / markets where licensees and distributors are present (this is discussed in more detail at paragraph 3.6 below) / markets with bricks and mortar presence will nearly always need to be covered

- New gTLDs and new ccTLDs are constantly being launched – either as a New gTLD completes the application process, as IDNs of existing ccTLDs are delegated or as ccTLDs for newly created countries are being delegated for the first time. Brand owners should keep an eye on these developments in case any New gTLDs or new ccTLDs are of interest

- Other relevant ccTLDs might be related to future expansion plans / markets which are hard to police (e.g. *.cn*; *.ru*) / markets where infringers are active / ccTLDs in which it is free to register (e.g. *.tk*)

The take home message here is that there is no one size-fits-all approach for domain registration strategy and every business will have different needs and considerations. Make sure that there is a valid commercial rationale for having each domain registration in the portfolio and do not be tempted to go for an indiscriminate wholesale registration approach.

3.2 Thorough searches before choosing your domain

When registering a domain as part of a new venture, it is prudent to carry out searches before settling on the domain name. The results of these searches should not only highlight any serious issues with earlier third-party rights but would also be valuable evidence of legitimate interest or other good faith intent in the event of a dispute in the future.

It is likely that for any sufficiently important launch full trade mark availability searches will already have been carried out. A trade mark is the most likely right for complainants to rely on in disputes (be it related to the corresponding domain name or in respect of the use more generally) and having a thorough understanding of the third-party landscape is vital.

These trade mark searches, however, are only part of the picture when considering possible domain name disputes.

Trade marks by their nature are jurisdictionally limited and are tied to specific goods and services by the wording of their classification. Domain names are neither limited in geographical scope nor in respect of what goods and services they can be used in relation to. The ccTLDs are each connected to their own jurisdiction but it is perfectly possible, for example, to access a *.co.uk* domain and make a purchase whilst outside of the UK.

The result of this is that the registration of a domain name, even if it is in a ccTLD, can potentially give rise to a dispute with a complainant from anywhere on the globe. It is not determinative that the domain registrant might have no intention of trading in the complainant's home jurisdiction or in any jurisdiction in which it has earlier rights.

This creates a scenario where mitigating the potential legal risk of registering a domain name through searching far outweighs the cost of securing the registration itself. It is clearly neither feasible nor cost effective to carry out exhaustive global searches before registering a domain name. However, that does not mean that no searching should be done at all. It is certainly proportionate to supplement any trade mark availability searches with general Internet searches in particularly key markets and not to limit these by any particular goods or services.

Note that some full trade mark availability searches focus only on the relevant trade marks registers. In such a case any supplementary searches should encompass other rights that might form the basis of a dispute, such as Geographical Indications or company name registrations.

General Internet searches will also allow a potential registrant to assess whether any third party might be able to claim common law rights in a name or whether the owner of a registered trade mark might be able to assert extended rights on the basis of a large reputation.

If the searches uncover a potential problem in a jurisdiction that is not an important market, then it might be enough to forestall a dispute if the domain is made inaccessible to web users from that jurisdiction. Of course, this type of proactive action will only be possible if you have done enough searching to uncover the existence of the third-party issue in the first place.

One further relatively quick and simple search to carry out is to check whether the domain name that is intended to be registered has ever been the subject of a previous dispute. All domain name dispute decisions are published online and the websites of the various dispute resolution providers have case law databases searchable by disputed domain name.

This search is an important one and is particularly relevant when purchasing a domain from a third party or registering a domain that has (recently) lapsed. This is because registering/purchasing the intended domain name creates a new set of facts with a new material date that could reignite the dispute and allow any earlier complainant the opportunity to re-file their complaint.

3.3 Use invented words

There is an inherent tension between marketing motives that push for descriptive brands where the consumer is easily educated as to the nature of the product and the legal enforcement of those brands which pushes for the use of distinctive trade marks.

It will not always be practical to choose an invented word but it is worth noting that complainants that own trade mark registrations for invented words find it much simpler, quicker and cheaper to succeed when domain disputes arise.

Savvy cybersquatters are aware of this and it could nudge them into choosing a different target whose brand sits much lower down the spectrum of distinctiveness and for which they might just be able to get a dispute decision in their favour. This would of course put the cybersquatter in a much stronger position in any subsequent negotiation to purchase the domain.

The recent *WIPO UDRP Case D2025-0940 <divebuddyapp.com>* is an example of a complainant failing in its UDRP action, despite the disputed domain being highly similar to the name in which it was claiming rights, as that name was deemed too descriptive to be enforceable.

Conversely, the recent *WIPO UDRP Case D2025-3108; <velux.one>* is an example of a complainant succeeding easily in its UDRP action. The panel considered that it was not credible that the domain name could have been chosen in ignorance of the complainant's very distinctive rights.

3.4 Register your trade marks

Although it will not be possible in all circumstances, it is advisable for the domain name to correspond to a registered trade mark in the ownership of the domain name registrant.

Cybersquatters will often check the registers to see if the brand that they are proposing to target has in fact been registered as a trade mark. Brand owners can, therefore, avoid some of the risk of cybersquatting by ensuring that their key brands are protected by registered trade marks and thus not appearing to be a soft target.

From the Respondent perspective, being able to exhibit a trade mark registration certificate corresponding to the domain name would be good evidence that the domain is proposed to be used for a legitimate business. Panels are reluctant to order transfer of domains in those circumstances and often hold in favour of the respondent saying that the parties would be better served by conducting infringement proceedings in the courts.

Most complainants research a potential respondent before launching a dispute and the existence of a registered trade mark (or other indication of legitimate activity) may well be enough to stop them from commencing the dispute in the first place.

3.5 Timing of domain registration

A follow-on point from making sure that trade marks are registered is not to leave too much time between filing the application for trade mark protection and the registration of domain name. Ideally, these steps should either be taken at the same time or the domain name should be registered as a first step.

Applications for trade marks are a matter of public record and cybersquatters have been known to watch the trade marks registers in the hope of snapping up corresponding domain names which the trade mark applicant has failed to register themselves. See by way of example *Nominet DRS D00019621 <cybfx.co.uk>*.

3.6 Licensees and distributors

Many modern businesses rely on networks of licensees and distributors to achieve global reach. It frequently creates problems when such licensees and distributors register in their own name domain names relating to the rights owner's product.

Many ccTLDs are restricted and will only allow certain categories of entity to register domain names. Ownership of (an application for) a registered trade mark in the relevant jurisdiction (e.g. *.au*) or a local representative/address for service (e.g. *.de*) is sometimes sufficient. This allows brand owners to register domains directly. However, some registries are stricter and a physical presence in the jurisdiction or a local tax ID (e.g. *.br*) is needed.

In such circumstances it could make sense for the licensee or distributor to register the domain name but the overarching agreement should make it clear that the domain is held on trust for the brand owner.

Rights owners should ensure that agreements are crystal clear on the following points:

- who is to be the registrant for any domain names associated with the business arrangement;
- any restrictions in place on the licensee's or distributor's ability or register domains and/or bring any associated domain name dispute actions;
- that all domains ultimately belong to and are held on trust for the rights owner; and
- the mechanism by which any domains are to be transferred into the ownership of the rights owner in the event that the business relationship comes to an end.

3.7 Active portfolio management

Many disputes arise due to simple missed deadlines or incorrect contact data because brand owners have a fragmented approach to domain registration and domain portfolio management.

Brand owners should ensure that at the earliest opportunity, and ideally before a dispute arises, they create a policy for how domain names are to be registered, used and maintained.

Such a policy should consider/include:

- Identifying which part of the business is to be in charge of domain name issues (e.g. is it to be IT or legal?);
- Identifying a single entity that should own the domains so that consistent registrant details can be used across the board;
- Keeping registrant contact details up to date;
- Keeping an accurate database of who owns which domains and when the next renewal falls due;

- Prohibition on *ad hoc* registrations;
- Appointing an in-house domains champion / super-user who is to be the first point of contact for all domain related questions;
- Categorising domains into top, medium and low priority and have different transfer or lapsing procedures for each category;
- Periodic reviews and audits, ideally every year, to see if any domains can be lapsed and ensure that portfolio is streamlined;
- Multi-year registration for key domains;
- Single year registration for less important domains;
- Setting key domains to auto-renew;
- Using "locks" at the registrar to prevent accidental transfer or lapse;
- Using a corporate registrar rather than a retail registrar;
- Linking any domains held in ccTLDs that have a trade mark registration requirement to the supporting trade mark so that it is not allowed to lapse or be assigned separately of the domain name;
- Setting up a domain watching service to monitor new third-party registrations;
- Creating a specific policy around enforcement issues;
- Making sure all employees are aware of the policy and knows that it needs to be followed; and
- Ensuring that licences and distribution agreements refer to and incorporate the policy.

3.8 Litigious reputation

Seasoned trade mark practitioners well know that there are a number of businesses that take a very protective stance with their intellectual property. This experience allows advisors to forewarn clients when, for example, a particular trade mark application is likely to face objections even if the technical legal position is such that those objections might fail in the long run. In some cases this is sufficient for the client to opt for an alternate name that might have a smoother run toward eventual registration.

Similarly, in the domain name environment, where all dispute decisions are freely available online, a litigious reputation might just persuade a savvy cybersquatter to seek a softer target elsewhere.

3.9 Defensive domain registrations

There are two opposing schools of thought on defensive domain registrations.

The first (and most common) viewpoint is that a defensive domain registration has no value as it only prevents registration of the *exact* domain in the *exact* TLD. Given the vast number of ways to circumvent such a narrow block, a huge number of domains will inevitably remain unprotected. Accordingly, a proponent of this view would say that it is pointless to take on the cost and administrative burden of maintaining a defensive portfolio at all and that disputes should just be dealt with if and when they arise.

The second viewpoint is that domain name disputes are relatively expensive to prosecute and if even only one dispute is avoided then that will justify the maintenance of a defensive portfolio. Of course, if more than one dispute is avoided then a larger defensive portfolio would be justified. It is perhaps also easier to obtain budgetary approval for the maintenance of a domain portfolio (which can be seen as an asset overall) rather than legal fees for dealing with disputes (which are pure overhead). Proponents of this view often maintain portfolios of many thousands of defensive registrations. They tend to be large corporations whose products are at high risk of infringement (e.g. cigarette manufacturers).

There is no one size fits all approach on this issue and for nearly all businesses the reality will be somewhere on the spectrum between these two extremes. Provided that a strategy has been carefully thought out and followed, a targeted number of defensive domain registrations would be appropriate in most cases.

The starting point when creating a defensive strategy should be following the same considerations as discussed above when protecting an existing portfolio. That is to say, you should narrow down the scope of the exercise by focussing on key brands and markets including where products are sold, manufactured or where licensing/distribution agreements are in place.

It is a helpful thought experiment to consider the likely reaction to a hypothetical third-party domain name registration. For example, as the owner of *brand.com* and *brand.co.uk*, what action would be required in response to third-party domain registrations for *brand-uk.com*, *brand-ltd.co.uk*, *brand-fakes.com*, *ilovebrand.co.uk*, *brand.de* or *brand.xxx*?

If the answer is that a domain name dispute would *certainly* need to be filed, then it makes sense to include that domain name within a defensive portfolio. Conversely, if the action would depend upon the other circumstances of the matter (or indeed that no action was needed at all), then the domain does not need to be proactively blocked by a defensive registration.

If after having gone through the thought experiment the list of defensive registrations is very large then this will need to be balanced against the commercial realities of maintaining such a portfolio. Being so defensive that your business sinks under the weight of the domain name portfolio is clearly not going to be a good idea. This is particularly the case when even a very large defensive portfolio can be easily circumvented by an ill-intentioned respondent.

3.9.1 Mergers and joint ventures

Imminent large corporate issues such as mergers and joint ventures have been fertile ground for domain name disputes over the years. This is an area where a little prior thought and a cheap defensive domain name portfolio can potentially save a lot of time and effort.

The case *Glaxo plc v Glaxowellcome Ltd (1996) FSR 388* is one in a long series that in fact relate to company name registrations. The judicial approach in these cases has been directly applied to domain name cases, however. The company name Glaxowellcome Ltd was registered shortly after Glaxo plc announced its intention to take over Wellcome plc. The company never traded but was offered for sale to Glaxo plc for £10,000. Lightman J granted a *quia timet* injunction on the grounds of passing off. The decision of Laddie J in *Direct Line Group v Direct Line Estate Agency Ltd [1997] FSR 374* is also a notable example of this type of case.

Similarly, *Global Projects Management Ltd v Citigroup, Inc. & Ors [2005] EWHC 2663 (Ch)* concerned the merger of Citicorp, Inc. and Travelers Group Inc. to create Citigroup, Inc. The announcement of the merger took place on the morning of 6 April 1998 and Global Projects Management Ltd registered the domain name citigroup.co.uk that same afternoon. Park J gave summary judgment in favour of Citigroup on both passing off and trade mark infringement.

More recently, in *WIPO UDRP Case D2017-0438* and *Nominet DRS Case D00018607*, J Sainsbury plc were required to commence domain name dispute proceedings in respect of a total of 10 domain names being variations of *<sainsburyargos.com>* and *<sainsburysargos.co.uk>*. The respondent registered the various domains on and around 5 February 2016, shortly after the acquisition of Home Retail Group (being the parent company of Argos Limited) by J Sainsbury plc had been announced in the media. The panels in both the WIPO and Nominet proceedings ordered transfer of the domains.

It can be seen from the above cases that the rights owner was successful every time. However, even a very strong case still stakes time, effort and money to prosecute to a successful completion. A much smaller outlay on a defensive domain portfolio could have prevented these disputes.

3.9.2 Typosquatting and spoofing risks

It is sensible to include within a defensive portfolio any domain name which is an obvious typosquatting or spoofing target.

Typosquatting refers to a particular form of cybersquatting in which the domain registrant seeks to attract Internet traffic to a website by using second level domain letter strings incorporating common typographical errors of popular brands or other search terms. For example, a typosquatter might register the domain names <mocrosoft.com> or <gooogle.com> in an attempt to capture web traffic intended for <microsoft.com> or <google.com>.[12]

Spoofing (also known as a homograph attack) is a further variation in which the domain registrant seeks to confuse Internet users by registering second level domain letter strings that are visually similar to (but not actually typographical errors of) popular brands or other search terms. For example, a spoofer might register the domain names <rnicrosoft.com> or <goog1e.com>. This might be done either to drive web traffic or to perpetrate email scams.

The rise of the scammer has meant that spoofing is becoming an increasingly common phenomenon in the modern Internet. The technique is frequently observed in phishing cases and the risk is particularly apparent for Internet users browsing on smartphones and tablets where the full URL of a website is often hidden or only visible in a very small font size.

When the DNS was first created only the ASCII characters a-z, 0-9 and the hyphen were permitted to be used. This provided a limited number

12 A recent example is *WIPO UDRP Case No. D2025-2094 <tglfriday.com>*

of opportunities for spoofing which were relatively easy to spot if sufficient attention was being paid. Common examples were:

- the conjoining of the letters “r” and “n” (i.e. “rn”) to look like the letter “m”;
- the conjoining of two letter “v”s (i.e. “vv”) to look like the letter “w”;
- the conjoining of the letters “c” and “l” (i.e. “cl”) to look like the letter “d”;
- the lowercase letter “i” can look like the lowercase letter "l"; and
- the numbers "0" and “1” can look like the capital letter "O" and the lowercase letter "l", respectively.

In the present-day DNS Internationalized Domain Names (IDNs) and domain names using Punycode are allowed.

IDNs can use a wide range of non-Latin and special characters from different languages. Punycode is an algorithm used to transform non-Latin and special characters into an ASCII-compatible string. For example, the IDN málaga.com would be written as <xn--mlaga-xqa.com> in Punycode.

Web browsers and email clients automatically decode Punycode so that Internet users see the domain name in the plain text incorporating the non-Latin and/or special character.

This enables registrants to register domain names consisting of or containing letters and characters from numerous non-Latin alphabets and Latin alphabets which contain accents.

Whilst the addition of these different characters and scripts enables non-English speaking web users to navigate the Internet in their local language, it has opened the door to a great many more opportunities for spoofing which are much harder, if not impossible, to spot. By way of example, the letter "ο" (a Greek alphabet *omicron*) is visually indistinguishable from the Latin letter "o".

It is beyond the scope of this book to go into the full detail of the types of spoofing being encountered. However, the table below shows a small number of some commonly-spoofed letters which highlights the point that, even if very close attention were to be paid, it would be difficult to realise that the domain name was not what it appeared to be.

Latin Character/Number	Spoof Character/Number
	Cyrillic alphabet
a, c, e, o, p, x, y	а, с, е, о, р, х and у
3, 4 and 6	З, Ч and б
	Greek alphabet
o, nu	ο and "nu"
	Armenian alphabet
o, n, u, S, L	օ, ո, ս, Տ and Լ
	Accents
google.com	google.com
i	ï, ì, í

Two examples of homograph spoofing are *WIPO UDRP Case No. D2013-1318 <sıemens.com> [xn--semens-p9a.com]* in which the registrant used the Turkish alphabet character letter "ı" in place of the Latin alphabet character "i" and *WIPO UDRP Case No. D2025-1453 <guccĩ.com> [xn--gucc-jya.com], <guccī.com> [xn--gucc-tya.com], <guccï.com> [xn--gucc-8pa.com], <guċċi.com> [xn--gui-7paa.com],*

<ġucci.com> [xn--ucci-9wa.com] in which the registrant used various non-Latin characters to replace the Latin alphabet characters "i", "c" and "g". In both cases, the panel had no difficulty in finding that the disputed domain names had been registered and used in bad faith.

ICANN is alive to the risk of spoofing and is consulting on ways that this might be addressed without unnecessarily restricting the use and availability of IDNs.

Punycode and non-Latin and/or special characters are not permitted in .uk but Nominet does allow IDNs in the *.wales* and *.cymru* ccTLDs[13] under certain conditions.

EUR*id*, the registry for the *.eu, .ею and .ευ* ccTLDs has had a no script mixing rule since June 2019 following its adoption of the IDNA2008 standard.[14] The alphabet used in the SLD must correspond to the alphabet of the ccTLD. This is straightforward as regards the *.ею* and *.ευ* ccTLDs. However, domain names using Punycode can still be registered in the *.eu* ccTLD so a risk of homograph spoofing remains.

3.10 Register your own TLD

A further option for avoiding disputes, although out of the reach of most businesses on cost grounds, would be to register a new gTLD for exclusive use by that business.

The TLD owner would have control of all of the second level domain names in the register and this, of course, would make cybersquatting in that register impossible.

---

13 https://registrars.nominet.uk/wp-content/uploads/2019/06/CymruWalesIDNPolicy_0.pdf

14 https://eurid.eu/en/knowledge-centre/domain-names-with-special-characters-idns/

As we discuss in Chapter Four, the second round of new gTLDs is underway. Any business considering this option would be well advised to begin the planning process without delay.

3.11 Conclusion

The key take home message for this chapter is that, whilst the risk cannot be removed entirely, a little thought and planning can go a long way to reducing the likelihood of encountering a domain name dispute. It is key to draft a policy and then make sure that it is actually disseminated amongst employees and adhered to.

There is no one size-fits-all approach and every business will have different requirements and priorities.

CHAPTER FOUR

NEW GTLDs

In 2011 the domain name system contained only 22 gTLDs and, as Internet usage became ubiquitous, the lack of domain names that were both desirable and available was beginning to pinch. In response to pressure from business, and with a view to encouraging more innovation, competition and consumer choice, ICANN launched a program to expand greatly the DNS by allowing the creation of New gTLDs.

When the deadline for the first application round closed in April 2012, a total of 1,930 applications for New gTLDs had been submitted. Some popular strings were the subject of multiple applications (such as *.app*, *.web* and *.law*) but approximately 1,400 were for unique strings.

Roughly 600 of the new gTLDs which have been delegated (i.e. introduced to the Internet) are for *.[brand]* letter strings with the remainder being for geographic or other generic terms. Examples are *.bmw*, *.london* and *.restaurant*.

The first New gTLD went live in October 2013. The 1,000th New gTLD went live in May 2016.

There was no real restriction on who could apply to create a New gTLD and any established corporation, organisation or institution in good standing was eligible. However, the application process was tortuous and the official fee payable to ICANN for submitting the application was set at a prohibitive USD 185,000. Anecdotally, applicants on average required a total investment in the region of USD 500,000 before their New gTLD was successfully delegated.

Applications could be standard (i.e. strings corresponding to a trade mark or generic term) or on behalf of a community (i.e. strings corresponding to a term by which that community is known).

4.1 Current status of the first round

The current status of the first round is shown in the table below and it can be seen that since its launch (and as at 31 August 2025) the total number of delegated New gTLDs stands at 1,241 with 4 New gTLDs still proceeding through the application process.

Application Statistics: Overview	
Total Applications Submitted	1,930
Completed New gTLD Program (gTLD Delegated – introduced into Internet)	1,241
Application Withdrawn	646
Applications that Will Not Proceed/Not Approved	39
Currently Proceeding through New gTLD Program	4

Many of the delegated New gTLDs for *.[brand]* are still not yet in use or are in use only to redirect traffic back to the main company website at a legacy gTLD or ccTLD. This suggests that many New gTLDs were obtained primarily defensively or with only nebulous plans for future use in mind.

A further reason for the slow migration over to a *.[brand]* New gTLD may be that many anti-phishing training programmes warn users to be wary of emails, links and websites that employ uncommon TLDs. Certainly brand owners would not want to do anything that would deter consumers from visiting their websites or reading their email correspondence.

No doubt usage of *.[brand]* New gTLDs will pick up as public awareness grows and when the marketing, security and data gathering benefits of using them begin to hit home.

4.2 The second round

Businesses which either missed the boat or decided not to submit applications in the first application round have successfully lobbied ICANN to launch a second round. There will likely also be third and fourth (and more) rounds in the future as the brand landscape is ever-changing and there will be no shortage of applicants.

The formal application submission period is expected to open in April 2026. The Applicant Guidebook setting out all the details for applications is expected to be published by December 2025.

For this second round ICANN has also launched an Applicant Support Program[15] offering financial and non-financial assistance to smaller applicants to make the process of applying for and operating a new gTLD more accessible. The window for applications to the Applicant Support Program is currently expected to close on 19 November 2025.

In addition to the Applicant Support Program, the key differences between the first and second rounds are likely to be:

- Contention resolution changes to ensure that applicants genuinely intend to operate the gTLD applied for. Including the opportunity for applicants to have a back-up letter string within their application.

- IDN new gTLDs will be allowed in Arabic, Armenian, Bangla, Chinese (Han), Cyrillic, Devanagari, Ethiopic, Georgian, Greek, Gujarati, Gurmukhi, Hebrew, Japanese (Hiragana, Katakana, and Kanji [Han]), Kannada, Khmer, Korean (Hangul and Hanja [Han]), Lao, Latin, Malayalam, Myanmar, Oriya, Sinhala, Tamil, Telugu, and Thai.

---

15 https://newgtldprogram.icann.org/en/application-rounds/round2/asp

- Creation of a Predictability Framework to increase efficiency and transparency when examining the applications.

- Creation of a Registry Service Provider (RSP) Evaluation Program to simplify the examination process by separating out the ability to operate the gTLD registry from the acceptability of the gTLD letter string itself.

Applicants will need to review the finalised Applicant Guidebook once it has been published to see full details on the revised application procedure rules.

4.3 The Trademark Clearing House

When the first new gTLD round was being contemplated, brand owners voiced their understandable concerns that the creation of so much new Internet real estate could lead to an explosion in cybersquatting activity.

To address those concerns ICANN created a new independent organisation called the Trademark Clearing House[16] in March 2013.

The TMCH is a centralised repository of verified trade mark rights from all over the world. The trade mark data it contains is used to support rights protection mechanisms relating to the second level domains in all new gTLDs.

The TMCH is divided up into two functions – the first of which is the authentication and verification of trade mark records and the second of which is the storage and dissemination of this data to the new gTLD registries so that they can operate their rights protection mechanisms.

Rights can undergo either a basic or an advanced validation assessment. Owners of the former category of validated right are entitled to use of the Trademark Claims service and the Ongoing Notifications service.

16 https://trademark-clearinghouse.com/

Owners of the latter category of validated right are in addition issued with a unique authentication key known as a Signed Mark Data (SMD) file which provides access to the Sunrise service, Blocking services and proves the existence of the right for the purposes of filing domain disputes via the Uniform Rapid Suspension System (see Chapter 8).

Access to a specific sunrise period would be available even if the right is not on the TMCH database but the rights holder would need to undergo a separate registry validation process in each case. Therefore, obtaining a validated TMCH record and SMD file can save a great deal of time and effort if domain name registrations are likely to be required in multiple new gTLDs.

The application fee structure is currently set at USD 155 for one mark for one year, USD 465 for one mark for three years and USD 775 for one mark for five years. Bulk discounts are available.

The TMCH is not an open register and it no longer publishes statistics on the number of rights registered on its database. The final statistics update released in 14 May 2019 showed 45,154 rights registered in the TMCH comprising trade marks from 117 countries and 131 jurisdictions. The figure today is likely to be in the region of 50,000-55,000 rights.

Given that there are millions of live trade mark registrations in the UK and EU alone, it is clear to see that only a small fraction of global trade mark owners have availed themselves of the TMCH and its services.

4.3.1 Eligibility and registration process

Any registered trade marks, any marks protected by statue or treaty, any court-validated marks as well as any other marks that constitute Intellectual Property (e.g. common law trade marks) rights are eligible for inclusion in the TMCH.[17]

17 Trademark Clearinghouse Guidelines March 2024, Version 1.3, section 2;

Each of these categories of rights has its own definition and eligibility criteria. The focus here is on registered trade marks as these are the most common rights lodged in the TMCH.

The TMCH defines registered trade marks as national or regional (i.e. multi-national) trade marks registered on the principal register and having national or multi-national effect at the time the application for verification is made. Pending applications, registered trade marks with sub-national effect or revoked registrations are specifically stated not to be eligible.[18]

The application must include the relevant details of the mark so that they can be independently validated. These include,[19] for example, an indication of the mark itself, registration number, registration date, jurisdiction, list of goods and services and the name, address and status of the trade mark holder.

The application is to be filed either by the trade mark holder directly or by a Trade Mark Agent acting on its behalf. Trade Mark Agent in this context does not mean a Chartered Trade Mark Attorney or IP solicitor but a third-party company that has applied to the TMCH for the right to become an agent and to act on behalf of trade mark holders. The annual fee for becoming a Trade Mark Agent is currently set at USD 5,000 for the Silver tier and USD 15,000 for the Gold tier.

4.3.2 Trade Marks Claims Service

Rights which have passed through the basic validation assessment are entitled to be enrolled on the Trade Marks Claims Service scheme.

---

https://trademark-clearinghouse.com/wp-content/uploads/2024/04/Trademark-Clearinghouse-guidelines-new.pdf

18 ibid; section 2.2.1

19 ibid; section 2.2.2

During at least the first 90 days of the general availability period of any new gTLD, persons attempting to register a domain name which corresponds exactly to a trade mark record on the TMCH database will receive a notification that their proposed domain name potentially conflicts with third-party IP rights.

The domain name registration process can only be finalised once the domain applicant acknowledges receipt of the notification, confirms that it understands its content and states that to the best of its knowledge it will not infringe the trade mark rights listed in the notice.

If such an acknowledgement is not received then the domain registration does not proceed. If after having received the notification the domain applicant decides not to proceed then that domain name remains unregistered.

If the domain applicant does choose to continue with its registration then the rights holder is notified. The rights holder can then commence a UDRP case, a URS case or other dispute mechanism, if necessary.

After the initial 90-day period ends, rights owners continue to receive notifications at no additional cost through the Ongoing Notifications service. Notifications are issued when a domain corresponding exactly to the TMCH record is registered. Rights owners can also include at no cost variations[20] of the TMCH record which will catch domains which wholly or partially contain the trade mark and similar domains which use common spoofing characters.

The Ongoing Notifications service is purely reactive and the domain registrants neither receive any notification nor have to acknowledge the earlier trade mark rights.

As of November 2018 there have been 272,323 TMCS notifications and 867,425 ongoing notifications sent to brand owners.

20 https://trademark-clearinghouse.com/variants/

At first glance one might think that this Trade Marks Claims service notification procedure is going to be largely ineffective as all a potential domain applicant would have to do is to indicate that it wants to proceed and it will be able to register its desired domain. However, the notification is deliberately worded such that anyone sending an acknowledgement and proceeding with the domain registration would not be able to claim in any subsequent UDRP or URS action that it was unaware of the trade mark owner's earlier rights. This makes it much, much easier to succeed in such an action as proving that the domain was registered in bad faith (i.e. it was registered in full knowledge of the existence of the earlier rights) is often the highest hurdle to overcome.

An independent review[21] of the TMCH's service of 23 February 2017 showed of roughly 1.9 million attempted domain name registrations there was a 94% abandonment rate after notification to the domain applicant and only a 0.3% dispute rate after notification of the rights holder (i.e. in cases where the domain applicant decided to proceed despite the notification).

The statistics suggest that the TMCS notifications are having a strong deterrent effect both on parties innocently attempting to register conflicting domains and on cybersquatters (who may realise they are likely to lose the domain in any subsequent UDRP action).

One might expect that a savvy cybersquatter would either continue with the registration of the domain and then transfer ownership to a different entity (i.e. to create a new effective registration date that was not tied to a notification) or simply wait until the initial 90-day period was over so as to avoid notification entirely.

---

21 Independent Review of Trademark Clearinghouse (TMCH) Services; Revised Report, section V.A.3; Jiarui Liu, Center for Internet and Society, Stanford Law School; University of San Francisco School of Law; Greg Rafert, Analysis Group; Katja Seim, The Wharton School, University of Pennsylvania

The report did not give any statistics regarding the transfer rate of domains that were registered after notification or the dispute rate after the 90-day period had ended. The report did state, however, that it found no evidence that that bad faith registrations were being timed strategically to avoid triggering notification.[22]

Nevertheless, the statistics show that the TMCS has had a significant positive effect on reducing the need to file domain name disputes and that in itself is a sufficient justification to register commercially important trade marks in the TMCH.

4.3.3 Sunrise periods

A sunrise period is a set length of time (usually 30 or 60 days) immediately after the launch of a new gTLD in which the registration of domain names is restricted only to holders of corresponding IP rights. Once the sunrise period is over the rights holder will have to compete for the domain name in the Limited Registration Period or register it on a first-come-first-served basis during the general availability phase.

The rationale for sunrise periods, therefore, is that they allow rights owners to buy up all domain names of interest before any cybersquatter can do so.

To access these sunrise periods a rights owner, in addition to the basic validation check, must submit to the TMCH evidence that its trade mark is in use. This must take the form of a signed declaration of use and a single sample of proof of use.

It is, of course, critical that brand owners take note of when such sunrise periods commence so that they can exercise their right of first refusal. Details of upcoming sunrise periods are published on the TMCH and ICANN websites.

---

22 ibid

It was noted above that brand owners have been slow to validate their rights with the TMCH and take advantage of sunrise periods. This may well be because the perception amongst brand owners is that the opportunity to register first is not particularly attractive when most domain strategies seek to avoid amassing large portfolios of defensive registrations that have no commercial value.

4.3.4 Blocking services

The TMCH appears to have understood the reluctance of brand owners to use sunrise periods and in response it has collaborated with third party businesses and registries to allow SMD validated TMCH records to access domain blocking services.

These blocking services allow brand owners to prevent the registration of domains corresponding to a record in the TMCH database *without* them having to register the domain themselves.

GlobalBlock, AdultBlock, DPML, NameBlock and ShortBlock are all accessible to rights owners who can provide a TMCH SMD file. Collectively, these services can block conflicting domain registrations in over 670 ccTLDs, gTLDs and new gTLDs. For the premium versions of these services it is also possible to include homograph and typo variants in the block and to block automatically any currently-registered conflicting domain which expires.

Blocking services are very much a step in the right direction and they are becoming increasingly popular with rights holders. It means that brands can be proactively defended without having to take on and maintain a bloated defensive portfolio.

4.6 Conclusion

The new gTLDs are here to stay with the second round due to launch in 2026. The program looks set only to grow larger with systemised applications likely in the years to come. This presents both opportunities and challenges to brand owners and to legitimate domainers.

One might expect the second (and subsequent) rounds of new gTLDs to be populated more by applications for *.brand* TLDs rather than for generic word or community-based word applications as many of these have already been snapped up.

Nevertheless, brand owners will need to have a clear understanding of their domain name strategy or else risk sinking under the burden of policing this ever-expanding Internet real estate.

CHAPTER FIVE

IS ACTION NECESSARY AND APPROPRIATE?

If none of the preventative measures discussed in the preceding Chapters work and an objectionable domain name is registered by a third party, what should you do next? Is it worth trying to negotiate first? Should you launch into the dispute all guns blazing or take a more considered approach?

The answer to these questions will be different in every case depending upon how seemingly innocuous or egregious the third party's actions are. However, the thought process that leads to the answer is the same in each case.

5.1 Pre-action correspondence

Not all registrants of objectionable domains are cybersquatters or scammers. Many intend to run genuine fansites or gripesites relating to the brand or simply just do not understand that they might be infringing or damaging IP rights by registering a domain name.

For this reason, a friendly first approach made via an anonymous third-party is nearly always worthwhile. It may well result in a transfer of the contested domain at much less time and expense than eventually succeeding in a dispute.

Although it would be tempting to take this pragmatic solution every time it is offered, care must be taken that registrants who have been acting in bad faith do not profit from their actions. If a brand owner develops a reputation as being one that will routinely pay a thousand pounds for the transfer of a domain then that brand owner may soon find that it is open season on its trade mark rights.

In cases where a brand owner suspects that the domain was registered in bad faith at the outset in order to get a quick payout then they would be well advised to proceed with a domain name dispute.

If the approach does not result in a transfer (e.g. because the domain is stated not to be for sale or because the brand owner decides not to pay the sum asked for), the initial correspondence with the domain registrant can nevertheless shed light on their motivations. This can be very helpful evidence for a complainant in any subsequent dispute.

In the absence of a transfer agreement, the next step is to send a Cease and Desist letter from or on behalf of the brand owner. This upping of the stakes may bring a wavering registrant round to the idea of transferring the domain – though not necessarily to the brand owner. It is not unheard-of for the registrant, upon receipt of such a letter, to revert to the third party that made the initial friendly approach and offer to sell them the domain and usually for a greatly reduced price.

If the Cease and Desist letter itself is unsuccessful, then the brand owner will have to decide whether or not the matter is sufficiently serious to warrant the commencement of a domain name dispute or court proceedings.

5.1.1 The without prejudice rule

As noted above, the comments of the registrant can potentially be helpful evidence for complainants in any dispute. This is the case even if the comments were made in without prejudice negotiations.

The UDRP Policy and Rules and the EUR*id* ADR Rules make no mention of the without prejudice doctrine at all. Numerous UDRP decisions[23] have specifically held that such correspondence can be taken

23 See by way of example, *WIPO UDRP Case No. D2023-4532* *<gucciancora.com>* & *WIPO UDRP Case No. D2021-1876,* *<webuyanyscania.com>*

into account on the basis that neither the panellists nor the parties may be familiar with the rule, it is an unnecessary complication and the efficacy of the Policy would be severely undermined if evidence which goes to the heart of the determination as to bad faith could be so easily excluded.

For similar reasons, the Nominet DRS Policy, at paragraph 11, states that without prejudice material "may" be considered by the Expert unless it was generated during the compulsory mediation stage or it is the Expert's belief that the material should be excluded "in the interests of justice". In general, without prejudice material will be admissible as evidence.[24]

If both parties are represented by Chartered Trade Mark Attorneys or solicitors then the parties could agree amongst themselves that any discussions are to be on a without prejudice basis. In effect the parties would be trusting each other's representatives to abide by their professional obligation to act ethically. It is unlikely ever to be safe to have without prejudice discussions with an unrepresented complainant or respondent.

Panellists are keen to dig down into the facts surrounding the registration of the domain name and the behaviour and intentions of the registrant. If the content of without prejudice discussions were to be filed in evidence, either by accident or by design, then they would certainly take them into account in their decision making if it would shed light on a party's motivations.

This makes it potentially very dangerous for the parties, and registrants in particular, to engage in pre-action correspondence. This is in no small part the reason why settlement approaches often go unanswered.

24 *Nominet DRS Case No. 00389, <scoobydoo.co.uk>; Nominet DRS Case No. D00023848 <webuyanyscania.co.uk>*

5.1.2 Threats to sue

If a Cease and Desist letter becomes necessary, a potential complainant might be tempted to broaden the scope of its letter also to allege trade mark infringement and passing off. This should be undertaken with caution.

Expressing the seriousness of the matter may prompt the registrant to an amicable resolution but it also opens the door to potential claim for unjustified threats[25] and a brand owner could find itself in court having to succeed on an infringement counterclaim in order to avoid liability.

Specifically in the context of the UDRP, paragraph 4(k) of the UDRP Policy states that the panel's decision will not be implemented by the registrar for ten business days so as to allow either party to commence related court proceedings if they were minded to do so. The panel's decision would be stayed until the court proceedings were resolved.

If the filing of a UDRP case would be a likely route in the event that the Cease and Desist letter does not resolve the matter, then complainants should consider writing a more targeted letter that does not allege trade mark infringement at all. In this way, the respondent would not have an obvious cause of action on which to hang related court proceedings and frustrate the prompt enforcement of the panel's decision.

5.2 Prioritising when to take action

It is generally not sufficient justification to launch a domain name dispute just because the domain should not have been registered. Emotional decisions should be avoided, focussing instead on any current and future business impact.

Factors to consider include:

25 Section 21 of the Trade Marks Act 1994

- How closely does the domain correspond to the rights (i.e. is it identical or an obvious typo)?
- Is the right in question particularly commercially important (i.e. is it a house mark or critical product brand name)?
- Is the domain required for your own business use?
- How is the domain being used by the registrant? Is the use causing:
    - confusion as to who owns the domain or associated website – for example, does the domain link to the brand owner's website or is the website selling the brand owner's own goods?
    - dilution or tarnishment to the brand – for example, is the website selling products related to brand owner's goods or poor quality competing products?
    - damage to the business – for example, is the website distributing counterfeit goods or illegal products?
- What are the chances of success?

5.3 Conclusions

If the brand owner cannot, or does not want to, take a transfer of the domain and the commercial position is such that a dispute is commercially justified, then the next step is to decide which dispute mechanism to use and launch the action.

PART C

DISPUTES

CHAPTER SIX

OVERVIEW OF THE DISPUTE RESOLUTION OPTIONS

If a brand owner finds itself in a position where it needs to take action against a domain then the first step is to determine which dispute resolution options are available to it and which is the most appropriate in the circumstances. This will depend upon the nature of the domain name itself and what use, if any, is being made of the domain name.

The most common options for brand owners would be:

- One of the various domain name alternative dispute resolution mechanisms
- Court action
- Registrar takedowns

6.1 Domain name dispute mechanisms

The domain name alternative dispute resolution mechanisms shown below are the most likely to be relevant to practitioners and brand owners in the UK.

- The Uniform Domain-Name Dispute-Resolution Policy ("UDRP")[26] – applies to all legacy gTLDs, all new gTLDs and around 44 ccTLDs

26 See Chapter 7 for the details

- The Uniform Rapid Suspension System ("URS")[27] – applies to all new gTLDs, the legacy gTLDs *.asia, .biz, .cat, .info, .jobs, .mobi, .museum, .org, .pro, .tel, .travel* and *.xxx* and the *.pw* ccTLD

- The Nominet DRS ("DRS")[28] – applies to the *.uk* ccTLD only

- The EUR*id* ADR ("ADR")[29] – applies to the *.eu, .ею* and *.ευ* ccTLDs only

It can be seen from this that the UDRP is by far the most common mechanism and is applicable to over 1,300 TLDs so far (with this number only set to grow) amounting to roughly 225 million domain registrations. Additionally, many of the ccTLDs which do not adopt the UDRP directly use it as the basis for their own individual systems.

The URS is applicable to over 1,250 TLDs so far but in absolute terms it much less widely applied than the UDRP as it does not cover the key *.com* or *.net* legacy gTLDs which make up approximately 46% of all registered domain names. It is also more limited than the UDRP as regards the types of dispute it can address.

The DRS applies to the *.uk* ccTLD in which there are roughly 10million domain registrations.

The ADR applies to the *.eu, .ею* and *.ευ* ccTLDs in which there are roughly 3.7million domain registrations in total.

Part C of this book focusses on the UDRP and then goes on to discuss the other domain name dispute mechanisms in a comparative fashion.

27 See Chapter 8 for the details

28 See Chapter 9 for the details

29 See Chapter 10 for the details

6.2 Court action

Whilst the various alternative dispute resolution mechanisms are likely to be the first port of call for resolving domain name disputes, the courts are always available for an appropriate case.

6.2.1 The UK legal landscape

The leading case on domain name disputes in the UK courts is *British Telecommunications Plc & Ors v One In A Million Ltd & Ors [1998] EWCA Civ 1272.*

One In A Million had registered various domain names incorporating the trade marks BT, BRITISH TELECOM, CELLNET, LADBROKES, SAINSBURYS, MARKS AND SPENCER and VIRGIN. The claimants brought actions for passing off and trade mark infringement and the judge at first instance granted summary judgment. It was held on appeal that:

- the mere registration of a domain name can amount to passing off as it makes a false representation that the domain registrant is associated or connected with the brand owner; and

- domain names consisting of well-known brands are instruments of fraud as any realistic use of them as domains would result in passing off; and

- the registration of the domain names also amounts to trade mark infringement under s.10(3) of the Trade Marks Act 1994. The domain names indicate trade origin and they were registered to take unfair advantage of the distinctive character and reputation of the marks.

There have been some subsequent decisions[30] of the CJEU which have cast doubt on whether the law on the s.10(3) trade mark infringement question remains applicable.

The first part of the passing off decision was based on the court's view that a WhoIs search would return results showing One In A Million as the domain owner and that this amounted to a misrepresentation that One In A Million was connected to or authorised by the trade mark owner.

A defendant might try to argue that the modern Internet user is more savvy and that, especially given the current WhoIs blackout, no misrepresentation as to connection or authorisation takes place and thus any goodwill the trade mark owner might have cannot be damaged by the registration of the domain name. However, the simple fact that a domain is registered and is owned by a company that has no right to the goodwill attaching to the domain name is likely to amount to passing off regardless of whether the domain is used in trade or if the consumer knows who owns that domain.[31]

In any event, the One In A Million case remains good law at the time of writing (particularly as it pertains to passing off and to domain names being instruments of fraud) and it has been relied on in numerous subsequent and more modern cases[32] from the Intellectual Property Enterprise Court ("IPEC"), to the High Court and the Court of Appeal.

---

30 *Céline SARL v Céline SA, Case C-17/06* and *L'Oréal SA v Bellure NV, Case C-407/07*

31 *Yoyo.Email Limited v Royal Bank of Scotland Group plc & Ors [2015] EWHC 3509 (Ch), at paragraphs 15 and 19*

32 See, by way of example, *Vertical Leisure Limited v Poleplus Limited [2014] EWHC 2077 (IPEC), Smithkline Beecham Limited & another v GSKLINE Ltd & another [2011] EWHC 169 (Ch)* and *Media Agency Group Limited and Transport Media Limited v Space Media Agency Limited and Ors [2019] EWCA Civ 712*

In *Vertical Leisure Limited v Poleplus Limited [2014] EWHC 2077 (IPEC)* the defendant had registered a number of domain names identical to the claimant's marks and then offered them for sale to the claimant. The IPEC declined to grant summary judgement on the s.10(3) trade mark infringement claim but did grant summary judgement on the claim for passing off. It ordered the domain names to be transferred to the claimant.

Summary judgement applications at the IPEC, whilst still more expensive and slower than a UDRP action, are not hugely so. It would certainly be a reasonable route for a rights owner to go down if the other party has been identified and there are no problems with the court's jurisdiction.

A summary judgement application should also be given careful consideration where there is a non-negligible risk at a respondent who has been unsuccessful in one of the domain name alternative dispute resolution mechanisms might commence related court action in an attempt to overturn or frustrate the decision to transfer ownership of the disputed domains.

The UK courts have been clear that they do not function as an instance of appeal from the UDRP/URS or of further appeal from the DRS. UK courts have also struck out requests to issue declarations that losing respondents are entitled to retain ownership of their domain names.[33]

Losing respondents have, however, had some moderate success in reaching settlements with complainants against the backdrop of US court proceedings.[34]

33 See, by way of example, *Michael Ross v Playboy Enterprises International, Inc. [2016] EWHC 1379 (IPEC)*, *Toth v Emirates & Anor [2012] EWHC 517 (Ch)* and *Patel v Allos Therapeutics Inc. [2008] E.T.M.R. 75*

34 *Yoyo.Email LLC v Playinnovation Limited, Arizona District Court, Case Number: 2:2014cv01922*

6.2.2 The US legal landscape

It is beyond the scope of this book to address in detail the legal position in the US. A few points are worthy of mention, however.

The US has enacted the Anti Cybersquatting Consumer Protection Act[35] specifically to deal with the practice of cybersquatting. It provides an effective route for plaintiffs and, with statutory damages of up to USD 100,000 per domain available, it has real teeth even when a domain has never been used.[36]

The US court accepts *in rem* jurisdiction over domain names where the registry, registrar or other authority is based in USA. This represents a very large proportion of all domain names as *.com*, *.net* and *.org* are all operated by registries in the USA and many of the largest registrars are US-based companies.

Procedures are available for mass seizure of domain names and US-located monies by means of interim court injunctions.

6.2.3 Court action vs UDRP

It is important to remember that trade mark infringement and the UDRP are two different beasts.

A complainant can succeed under the UDRP where a trade mark infringement action would be doomed to fail (for example because the respondent's use is not in the course of trade or the complainant has no rights in the respondent's jurisdiction).

Conversely, a trade mark infringement claim can succeed in situations where a UDRP action would be doomed to fail (for example, in

---

35 15 U.S.C. §1125(d)

36 *E. and J. Gallo Winery v. Spider Webs Ltd., 129 FSupp2d 1033 (S.D. Tex. 2001) aff'd., 286 F3d 570 (5th Cir. 2002)*

circumstances where a domain is being used for a legitimate business or was registered in good faith but is subsequently used in bad faith).

It is not appropriate, therefore, to view the UDRP as a cheaper mechanism for dealing with trade mark infringements on the basis that if a domain name can be taken away from a party then it will be forced into a total rebrand.

The factors to consider when deciding whether or not to commence court action or use the UDRP (or other mechanism) are:

- Jurisdiction
- Chances of success
- Costs
- Length of proceedings
- Remedies available
- Facts and evidence clear and easily presentable
- UDRP will not deal with website content

The UDRP is likely to be preferable to court action in most cases primarily as it is significantly quicker, simpler and cheaper (albeit that a summary judgement application at IPEC is closing the gap).

In addition, given the global nature of the Internet, there are very significant jurisdictional and enforcement advantages in using the UDRP. Panels have jurisdiction over all respondents whether they are UK-based or otherwise and even if they are unidentified. Enforcement of decisions is automatic regardless of the respondent's location.

The nature of the UDRP does make it unsuitable for certain cases, however.

Court action is likely to be the most appropriate route if the dispute has a complex factual background or if any of the factual matrix is disputed by the parties. Further, the UDRP deals with the domain name only and cannot be used to stop website content reappearing elsewhere. Courts can award injunctions as to website content and also offer other remedies such as damages and costs.

A potentially very significant advantage of court action is that the claimant has the choice of exactly when and where to launch proceedings. Users of the UDRP must submit to the jurisdiction of the courts in a "mutual jurisdiction" as defined under the UDRP Rules. For UK rights holder this will almost certainly be a foreign jurisdiction. There is a risk, therefore, that commencing a simple UDRP action could end up with the rights owner being a defendant in international litigation.

6.3 Registrar takedowns

Rather than using a judicial or quasi-judicial process to deal with abusive domain names, a rights owner can contact directly the registrar for the abusive domain and request that it is taken down. The registrar may agree to do this if the domain is being used in a way which breaches any terms in its registration agreement, in particular any acceptable use policy.

Each registrar will have their own conditions that need to be fulfilled before they will take down a domain name depending upon the specific terms of the registration agreement they have entered into with the domain registrant. However, almost all registrars will have a broad discretion to suspend or cancel a domain if it is used for any of the following types of activity:

- Breaches of UK or other law
- Hacking
- Botnets and DDoS attacks

- Distribution of malware and viruses
- Phishing or other fraudulent activity
- Sending spam email
- Web space abuse (e.g. illegal/obscene/threatening/ defamatory content on websites)
- Selling counterfeit goods and/or unauthorised copyright works
- Breaches of privacy

Any party can report such instances of misuse to a registrar whether or not it is their rights being targeted or their infrastructure that has been compromised.

If a brand owner becomes aware that any such activities are taking place in relation to its trade marks then immediate action will be necessary and the timescale of a UDRP action, or even a URS action, is likely to be too slow.

All ICANN-accredited registrars are obliged to provide contact information for receiving and dealing with reports of domain abuse and many will be keen to help if their infrastructure is being abused. Local laws in many countries also require registrars to take proactive steps to end such domain abuse once it is brought to their attention.

If the registrar is reluctant to take action or if there is particular urgency the matter can be escalated to any governmental or law enforcement bodies that have been specifically set up for tackling cybercrime.[37]

37 In the UK, options include the National Cyber Security Centre (https://www.ncsc.gov.uk/) and Action Fraud (https://www.actionfraud.police.uk/)

If the domain points to a website then the hosting company should also be contacted – though in many cases the registrar and the hosting company will be the same.

As can be seen from the above registrar takedowns are only appropriate in the most egregious cases and should not be used for cases of "normal" cybersquatting.

It is critical to have in place a domain monitoring service as action can only be taken against domains which have been highlighted as abusive.

A rights owner seeking a registrar takedown should make sure it distils all relevant information down into a clear report. This should as a minimum explain who is making the report and why, how urgent the matter is, how the criminal activity was discovered and what evidence there is to prove that it is taking place.

This report can then be sent to the relevant registrar's abuse team using the email address on its website (it is usually in the form *abuse@registrar.tld*) or by using the dedicated reporting form (if the registrar has set one up). It is recommended to follow up the initial report with a phone call.

The larger registrars have abuse teams that are permanently staffed so they can begin the takedown process as soon as it is reported to them.

6.4 Conclusion

Every dispute will have a range of available mechanisms. Deciding on which one to use is an important question.

The nature of the domain name, how it is being used and the identity and location of the domain registrant will all feed into the decision.

CHAPTER SEVEN

UNIFORM DOMAIN-NAME DISPUTE-RESOLUTION POLICY ("UDRP")

The UDRP is a contract-based alternative dispute resolution mechanism. It is intended to provide the owners of trade marks with a quick and cheap alternative to court litigation for addressing clear-cut cases of cybersquatting.

Its contract-based structure cuts out a great deal of complexity regarding international jurisdiction and enforcement issues that could potentially hamstring a claimant in court proceedings.

ICANN adopted the finalised text of the UDRP on 24 January 1999 following a global consolation process. WIPO was appointed as the first dispute resolution provider on 29 November 1999 and the first UDRP case was filed on 9 December 1999.[38]

The UDRP is applicable to over 1,300 TLDs and many of the specific ccTLD policies use it as their basis.

Verisign's Domain Name Industry Brief from Q1 of 2025[39] stated that there were roughly 225million domains registered across all gTLDs. WIPO's UDRP statistics can be extrapolated to reach a figure of roughly 100,000 UDRP cases filed in total across all providers thus giving a dispute rate of 0.04%. This is a very rough estimate but it nevertheless

38 *WIPO UDRP Case No. D1999-0001 <worldwrestlingfederation.com>*

39 https://blog.verisign.com/domain-names/verisign-q4-2017-domain-name-industry-brief-Internet-grows-332-4-million-domain-name-registrations-fourth-quarter-2017/

shows that the number of disputes is very low relative to the total number of registered domain names (albeit that it is climbing year-on-year).

The basic UDRP test is set out at paragraph 4(a) of the UDRP Policy. It states as follows:

> ***4(a) Applicable Disputes.*** *You are required to submit to a mandatory administrative proceeding in the event that a third party (a "complainant") asserts to the applicable Provider, in compliance with the Rules of Procedure, that*
>
> *(i) your domain name is identical or confusingly similar to a trademark or service mark in which the complainant has rights; and*
>
> *(ii) you have no rights or legitimate interests in respect of the domain name; and*
>
> *(iii) your domain name has been registered and is being used in bad faith.*
>
> *In the administrative proceeding, the complainant must prove that each of these three elements are present.*

The three elements of the test are cumulative and a complainant must demonstrate that, on the balance of probabilities, it has met the requirements in each in order for the complaint to be successful.

The basic procedure[40] of the UDRP is as follows:

1. Complaint filed with an ICANN-accredited provider chosen by the complainant (limited to 5,000 words excluding annexes)

40 UDRP Rules, paragraphs 3, 4, 5, 6, 15 and 16; UDRP Policy, paragraph 4(k); https://www.icann.org/resources/pages/udrp-rules-2015-03-11-en; https://www.icann.org/resources/pages/policy-2012-02-25-en

2. Formalities examination (and any filing deficiencies remedied within five days)

3. The provider notifies the appropriate registrar that a UDRP case has been filed and the domain is then "locked" so that it cannot be transferred into new ownership

4. The respondent is notified and then has 20 days to file its response. Failure to file a response will not result in default judgement in favour of the complainant

5. Appointment of an Administrative Panel (within five days)

6. Issuance of the Administrative Panel's decision (within 14 days)

7. ICANN and Registrar notified of decision (within three days)

8. Implementation of the Administrative Panel's decision by Registrar (within ten business days – subject to notification of commencement of court proceedings).

Each provider has its own Supplemental Rules regarding specific procedural issues (e.g. the timing of payment of the appropriate fees, requesting extensions of time and suspensions to allow settlement negotiations).

WIPO statistics show the average time to reach a decision is 60 days for cases involving a single panellist and 75 days for cases involving three panellists.

Panellists often grumble that they see far too many low quality pleadings and speculate that this might be because disputes are being taken too lightly or are not being allocated sufficient resources by complainants.

Regardless of whether or not this is true, it is certainly a good idea to get panellists onside at an early stage by writing a clear and concise pleading. The panellists get paid a flat fee for deciding cases and having to waste time deciphering a party's pleading must be frustrating indeed.

It is, therefore, in the interests of panellists and providers to educate potential users of the UDRP as to what type of claims and evidence they would like to see in certain situations. This results in faster and more consistent decision making and reduces the number of cases being brought which have no prospect of success.

WIPO puts a great deal of effort into education and regularly runs seminars and workshops for potential users of the UDRP.

7.1 The Providers and their differences

ICANN has contracted with five different bodies to provide UDRP services. These are:

- World Intellectual Property Organization("WIPO")
- Forum
- Czech Arbitration Court ("CAC")
- Asian Domain Name Dispute Resolution Centre ("ADNDRC")
- Canadian International Internet Dispute Resolution Centre (CIIDRC)

The International Institute for Conflict Prevention and Resolution ("CPR"), The Arab Center for Dispute Resolution ("ACDR") and eResolution are former providers who have now ceased offering UDRP services.

The table below shows the distribution of cases filed at the various providers since the creation of the UDRP:

Provider	Total no. of cases
WIPO	63,077
Forum	41,258
ADNDRC	3,441
CAC	5,369
CIIDRC	239
ACDR	~4
eResolution	276
CPR	151

The table shows that WIPO has been the chosen provider in roughly 57% of all cases.

It is estimated that a total of USD 600 million has been spent by brand owners since 1999 on prosecuting UDRP cases. This is a drop in the ocean of would have been spent had these roughly 110,000 cases all been decided in the courts.

Of all of the cases filed at WIPO since 1999 involving a single panellist, roughly 92% have resulted in the transfer (or cancellation) of the disputed domain. Of the remaining 8%, transfer was denied in roughly 6% of cases and the case was settled/terminated in roughly 2%.

Opponents of the UDRP often point to this statistic as evidence that the UDRP is biased in favour of complainants. This is not the case, however. The UDRP is designed for use in situations of obvious abuse of the DNS and the choice about whether or not to commence a UDRP action is entirely in the complainant's hands. Therefore, the system is self-selecting for cases which the complainant should win and it is unsurprising that UDRP cases are mostly successful. Indeed, ICANN and WIPO would prefer it if the denial rate were 0% as this would mean that complainants are not overreaching in their claims and the UDRP is being used as intended.

The UDRP filing statistics for 2024 show that WIPO was the chosen provider in 65% of cases. Forum received 25% of cases and the remaining 10% were shared amongst the other three providers.

Of the cases received by WIPO, the top three industry sectors were banking and finance (11%), retail (10%) and Internet and IT (10%).

It is also worth noting for UK-based legal representatives that the UK is the third most common jurisdiction for complainant location (accounting for 8% of cases) and respondent location (accounting for 6% of cases).

The providers are all different in terms of their cost and the panellists on their rotas. Knowing the characteristics of the respective providers is critical as the choice of provider can potentially have a significant outcome on their decisions in certain circumstances. The decision over choice of provider, therefore, is a tactical one and complainants should not just simply choose the provider that is the cheapest or most convenient.

This section focusses on the characteristics of WIPO, Forum and the CAC since these three providers account for the vast majority of cases and are likely to be the most relevant to a UK-based party.

WIPO and Forum are both excellent providers. The high throughput of cases means that the panellists are very experienced and hand down good quality and consistent decisions. In most cases, however, there are a number of reasons why WIPO will be the best provider to use.

Firstly, WIPO assists panellists in case management and decision proofreading. This makes it less likely that panellists might miss that a case is a re-filing or that the decision when issued contains errors (e.g. an incorrect party name or typos).

Secondly, WIPO allows for payment of the UDRP filing fee via the WIPO deposit account. Most UK law firms active in the IP field will have such an account in order to facilitate the filing of trade mark applications under the Madrid system. This makes WIPO administratively very easy to use.

Thirdly, WIPO is also the dispute resolution provider for the 44 ccTLDs listed below which have adopted the UDRP as their dispute resolution mechanism:

> *.ag, .ai, .as, .bm, .bs, .bz, .cc, .cd, .co, .cv .cy, .dj, .ec, .fj, .fm, .ga, .gd, .gt, .ki, .la, .lc, .md, .me, .mg, .mw, .nr, .nu, .pa, .pk, .pn, .pr, .pw, .ro, .sc, .sl, .sn, .so, .tj, .tt, .tv, .ug, .ve, .vg, .ws*

UDRP cases involving legacy gTLDs, new gTLDs and these 44 ccTLDs can be consolidated into a single action.

Fourthly, WIPO is more transparent about how it assigns cases to its rota of roughly 500 panellists. Although any considerations around how this is done are not fully public, WIPO has indicated that it considers the below points:

- Does the panellist have time to take the case on?
- Is the panellist facing a conflict of interest?
- Can the panellist understand the language of the proceeding?
- If both parties are from a particular jurisdiction, WIPO will try to appoint a panellist from that jurisdiction;
- If the parties are from different jurisdictions, WIPO will try to appoint a panellist from a neutral country; and
- Have any previous decisions of the intended panellist been cited in the complaint?

Some have suggested that the consideration in the final bullet point potentially gives complainants a means to steer WIPO away from appointing a particular panellist by citing their earlier decisions even if they are not particularly relevant to the matter at hand. No doubt, however, the case managers at WIPO are alive to this possibility and will not be unduly swayed by such practice.

The panellists at Forum are also appointed on a case-by-case basis but no detail as to how this is done has been released – though the same considerations as set out above are highly likely to factor into the decision.

The CAC first became a provider in 2009. It had only issued around 5,369 decisions as at 30 September 2025 but it is becoming increasingly popular. The complaint filing fee is broken up into two tranches – the first is for filing the complaint itself and the second becomes payable only if the case is defended (i.e. the respondent files a response). Even if both tranches need to be paid the total is significantly lower than the equivalent fee at WIPO or Forum.

The panellists are somewhat less experienced as there are fewer cases going through the CAC. However, the decision quality is still very good and some of the CAC panellists are also on WIPO's rota.

If the complaint is very strong and a response is unlikely to be filed then the CAC may well be the best provider to use.

The CAC may also be the appropriate forum in a situation where multiple complainants wish to consolidate their complaints against a single respondent.

There is no express provision under the UDRP Policy or Rules that allows for such consolidation. Panellists at WIPO have been willing to allow it[41] but the overarching principles are underdeveloped and there is a corresponding lack of certainty about how this type of consolidation request would be judged.

41 See by way of example *WIPO UDRP Case No. D2009-0331 <official-fulham-tickets.com>; Section 4.11.1, WIPO Overview 3.0*

The CAC, however, addresses this issue directly and Article 4(a) of its UDRP Supplemental Rules expressly provides for the filing of a "class complaint" by multiple complainants provided that:

- the legal arguments are applicable equally, or substantially in the same manner, to all the disputed domain names;
- the person representing the multiple complainants must prove that each of the complainants has authorised this; and
- the panel only orders the transfer of a disputed domain name to the relevant individual complainant that requested its transfer in the complaint.

The UDRP filing costs vary by provider, by the number of panellists and by the number of domain names in dispute. The filing costs for WIPO, Forum and CAC are set out in the tables below:

<u>WIPO costs breakdown</u>

Number of Domains	Single Panellist Fee (USD)	Three Panellists Fee (USD)
1-5	1,500 [Panellist: 1,000; WIPO: 500]	4,000 [Presiding Panellist: 1,500; Co-Panellists: 750; WIPO: 1,000]
6-10	2,000 [Panellist: 1,300; WIPO: 700]	5,000 [Presiding Panellist: 1,750; Co-Panellists: 1,000; WIPO: 1,250]
> 10	To be agreed with WIPO on a case-by-case basis	

These figures are flat rates and no additional fees are payable if panellists call for additional evidence on certain points or any other such procedural steps.

WIPO will refund a proportion of the filing fee equivalent to the panellist's fee if settlement occurs before a panel is appointed.

<u>Forum costs (breakdown of Forum fee vs panellist fee not available)</u>

Number of Domains	Single Panellist Fee (USD)	Three Panellists Fee (USD)
1-2	1,330	2,660
3 – 5	1,480	2,960
6 – 10	1,830	3,660
11 – 15	2,280	4,560
≥ 16	To be agreed with Forum on a case-by-case basis	

Additional fees are payable for extensions of time and other procedural steps.

<u>CAC costs</u>

Number of Domains	Single Panellist Fee (EUR)	Three Panellists Fee (EUR)	Additional UDRP Fees (EUR)
1-5	800 [Panellist: 400; CAC: 400]	2,600 [Presiding Panellist: 1,000; Co-Panellists: 500; CAC: 600]	300 [Panellist: 150; CAC: 150]
6–10	1,100 [Panellist: 600; CAC: 500]	3,200 [Presiding Panellist: 1,200; Co-Panellists: 600; CAC: 800]	400 [Panellist: 200; CAC: 200]

11–20	1,450 [Panellist: 850; CAC: 600]	3,800 [Presiding Panellist: 1,400; Co-Panellists: 700; CAC: 1,000]	500 [Panellist: 250; CAC: 250]
21–30	1,550 [Panellist: 850; CAC: 700]	4,400 [Presiding Panellist: 1,600; Co-Panellists: 800; CAC: 1,200]	600 [Panellist: 300; CAC: 300]
31–40	1,900 [Panellist: 1100; CAC: 800]	5,000 [Presiding Panellist: 1,800; Co-Panellists: 900; CAC: 1,400]	700 [Panellist: 350; CAC: 350]
41–50	2,000 [Panellist: 1100; CAC: 900]	5,600 [Presiding Panellist: 2,000; Co-Panellists: 1,000; CAC: 1,600]	800 [Panellist: 400; CAC: 400]
≥ 51	To be agreed with CAC on a case-by-case basis		

The Additional UDRP Fees are payable by the complainant within 5 days of notification by the CAC or the panel that an admissible response has been filed and that, based on the overall complexity of the case, the panel considers it is appropriate for the Additional UDRP Fees to be paid. Failure to pay the fees will result in the complaint being deemed withdrawn.

The CAC will issue partial refund of the filing fee if settlement occurs before a panel is appointed.

It can be seen from these fee schedules that cases can be heard by either a single panellist or a three-member panel. The majority of cases use only a single panellist and three person panels tend to be used only on more complex cases. Either party can request that the case is heard by three-member panel.

If the complainant's case turns on a minority view amongst panellists, then the respondent might tactically opt for a three-member panel so as to reduce the chance that the minority view will hold sway.

7.2 Contents of the complaint and the response

Much of the jurisprudence on the application of the three step UDRP test is now well established and this chapter does not discuss in detail those settled areas. Instead, it focusses on developing areas of jurisprudence and issues on which there is still some disagreement amongst panellists.

WIPO produces and maintains an extremely helpful overview of panel decisions[42] on the key UDRP requirements and other commonly disputed issues. It is now in its third iteration and should without a doubt be the starting point for any party filing a complaint or a response. This is true regardless of whether or not WIPO is the chosen UDRP provider.

WIPO also produces a Model Complaint[43] and a Model Response[44] for the benefit of the parties. Again, these are very useful regardless of whether or not WIPO is the chosen UDRP provider but they should be used with caution when a different provider has been chosen as some of the standard wording they contain is WIPO specific.

There is no strict doctrine of binding precedent under the UDRP but panellists will try to be consistent with previous decisions where possible so as to provide some legal certainty to the parties.

---

42 WIPO Jurisprudential Overview 3.0; https://www.wipo.int/amc/en/domains/search/overview3.0/

43 https://www.wipo.int/export/sites/www/amc/en/docs/complaint-lock-eudrp.doc

44 https://www.wipo.int/export/sites/www/amc/en/docs/response-lock-eudrp.doc

The most effective approach when drafting arguments is to start from the Jurisprudential Overview and then, if necessary, explain why the panellist should depart from its general rule in the particular case at hand. This will be much more persuasive than finding and relying on one obscure precedent that might support a tenuous point.

There is no limit on the number of trade marks that can be pleaded in a UDRP complaint but panellists will look favourably on a concise complaint that lists only three or four of the strongest rights. Of course, if more than three or four rights need to be pleaded in order to make the best case then complainants should do so.

The pleaded rights should include as a minimum the complainant's oldest word mark registration and the registration which is closest to the use the respondent is making of the domain. If available, the complainant should also include at least one trade mark registration from the respondent's home jurisdiction and any evidence of use of the mark supporting unregistered rights (in particular in the respondent's home jurisdiction).

If the portfolio of relevant registered rights is very large then they should be listed in an Annex. It is important that the panellist appreciates the size of the portfolio this is helpful *prima facie* evidence that the registrant must have been aware of the complainant and its rights at the time it registered its domain name.

Evidence of the respondent's activities used to support the pleadings should consist of screenshots rather than links. The respondent can control the content of the website and any links in the complaint may point to innocuous material by the time the panel comes to review them.

Using links to third-party content such as the Wayback Machine Internet archive is less risky though it is worth noting that the Wayback Machine only stores website text in its archive. If the archived page shows an image then this image originates from the webpage as it currently appears and, thus, can be manipulated by the domain registrant. If the image is important to any of the complainant's arguments then it would be prudent to rely on screenshots.

Complainants should search for the respondent in the UDRP/URS decisions database and, assuming this becomes possible again in the future, conduct reverse WhoIs and historic WhoIs searches. Previous adverse decisions against the respondent or their ownership of other domains containing third-party trade marks can be very good evidence of a pattern of abusive behaviour. If a pattern of abusive behaviour can be established then the complaint is much more likely to succeed.

The UDRP procedure does not guarantee the complainant the opportunity to file additional evidence or arguments even if the respondent files a response. Additional evidence and arguments can be submitted only at the panellist's request. Complainants should make sure, therefore, that the complaint is as thorough as possible and anticipates any arguments that the respondent might make as to legitimate interest under the second element.

If the respondent hinges its defence around an inconvenient fact that was ignored in the original complaint then the complainant's case will be significantly impaired.

In such circumstances the complainant could file additional evidence and try to get it admitted on the basis that it the response sets out new information that it did not know before the original complaint was filed. Such evidence provided unilaterally is often disregarded but it is clear the panellist will need to read it before deciding that it can be disregarded. It may give the complainant a small opportunity to influence the panellist's decision.

From a respondent perspective, the response should be fact heavy and brief and contain an explanation as to why they chose to register that particular domain.

If the respondent was not aware of the complainant's rights then this should certainly be mentioned as this points towards good faith intent at the time of registration. However, any respondent making spurious claims not to be aware of the complainant's rights in a very well-known trade mark will lose credibility and the panellist may then start to doubt the truthfulness of its other claims.

7.2.1 Who is the registrant?

This is a deceptively simple question.

ICANN adopts the technically legally correct approach that the registrant of a domain is whoever is listed in the "registrant" field on the WhoIs data (i.e. the other party to the contract with the registrar). However, this is very rarely the full picture and potential complainants often need to look deeper to uncover the true registrant of a domain.

In the present climate of WhoIs data being either abridged or not visible at all due to GDPR or the ubiquitous use of privacy services, it can be a challenge to dig down to the answer. Even if a registrant name is obtained this may not be the ultimate answer as, for example, a registrant may have used false details or company directors/employees may have filled out the registrant data incorrectly in their own names.

There are advantages to knowing the identity of the true registrant at an early stage as this party can then be named as the respondent in any dispute and this feeds into other issues in the UDRP assessment, in particular, the "commonly known by" ground of legitimate interest under the second element, the language of the proceedings and the choice of mutual jurisdiction.

Pushing too hard to identify the true registrant before filing the complaint can tip off the registrant and result in "cyberflight" (i.e. the ownership of the domain is transferred at the first sign of trouble so as to frustrate domain enforcement action).

Fortunately it is not critical to have the detail ahead of time and UDRP providers will allow a complaint to be filed with a privacy service as the respondent or with the respondent listed as "Name Redacted". The complaint can be subsequently updated once additional detail is known.

7.2.2 The language of the complaint

The default position is that the language of the proceeding is to be the language of the domain registration agreement.[45] This can be overridden by an agreement between the parties or the panel can rule that a different language should be used.

The UDRP provider will request confirmation of the language of the registration agreement from the relevant registrar when checking the complaint meets the filing formalities. If the complaint has been filed in a language other than that of the registration agreement, the complainant will be given the opportunity to translate it. For this reason it is usually best practice to include a request to change the language within the complaint itself.

Where there is no agreement over the language, the provider will communicate with the parties in both the language of the complaint and the language of the registration agreement. The panel will decide the language issue and set out its reasoning in the decision. If necessary, the complainant will be ordered to submit a translation of the complaint.

The circumstances[46] that may justify a change of language include:

- Evidence that the respondent can understand the language of the complaint – in particular if the parties have had prior correspondence in that language);
- The language and script of the domain name – in particular where this is the same as the complainant's mark;
- The content of any webpage visible at the contested domain – in particular the language of that content or other indicia such as addresses or currencies accepted;

45 UDRP Rules, paragraph 11(a)

46 WIPO Jurisprudential Overview 3.0, paragraph 4.5.1)

- The language of prior cases involving the respondent

- Any potential unfairness or delay caused by the need to translate the complaint

- Evidence of other respondent-controlled domain names being registered, used, or corresponding to a particular language

- In cases involving multiple domain names, the use of a particular registration agreement language for some (but not all) of the disputed domain names

This final bullet point can be very helpful in cases where the dispute includes consolidated gTLDs and ccTLDs and where the language of the registration agreement is likely to be different in each case.

The broad discretion under the UDRP Rules allows panellists the flexibility to address the issue of language in the best interests of achieving a prompt and fair result. An example of this in practice is *WIPO UDRP Case D2016-1273 <dececco.com>* in which the complainant and its representatives were Italian and the complaint was filed in English with a request that English be made the language of the proceeding. The respondent was Chinese and the registration agreement was in Chinese but the domain was in the Latin alphabet, the website visible at the disputed domain was in English and the respondent was represented by a firm of lawyers in Canada. The panel came to the view that it was entirely proper for English to be the language of the proceeding.

7.2.3 Mutual jurisdiction

The issue of mutual jurisdiction should be given special consideration by complainants and their representatives as it is a potential banana skin for a number of reasons.

Paragraph 1 of the UDRP Rules defines mutual jurisdiction as follows:

> ***Mutual Jurisdiction*** *means a court jurisdiction at the location of either (a) the principal office of the Registrar (provided the domain-name holder has submitted in its Registration Agreement to that jurisdiction for court adjudication of disputes concerning or arising from the use of the domain name) or (b) the domain-name holder's address as shown for the registration of the domain name in Registrar's Whois database at the time the complaint is submitted to the Provider.*

Paragraph 3(b)(xii) of the UDRP Rules states that:

> ***3. The Complaint***
>
> *(b) The complaint including any annexes shall be submitted in electronic form and shall:*
>
> *(xii) State that Complainant will submit, with respect to any challenges to a decision in the administrative proceeding canceling or transferring the domain name, to the jurisdiction of the courts in at least one specified Mutual Jurisdiction*

Paragraph 4(k) of the UDRP Policy in relevant part is as follows:

> ***4(k) Availability of Court Proceedings.*** *The mandatory administrative proceeding requirements set forth in Paragraph 4 shall not prevent either you or the complainant from submitting the dispute to a court of competent jurisdiction for independent resolution before such mandatory administrative proceeding is commenced or after such proceeding is concluded. If an Administrative Panel decides that your domain name registration should be canceled or transferred, we will wait ten (10) business days (as observed in the location of our principal office) after we are informed by the applicable Provider of the Administrative Panel's decision before implementing that decision. We will then implement the decision unless we have received from you during that ten (10)*

> *business day period official documentation (such as a copy of a complaint, file-stamped by the clerk of the court) that you have commenced a lawsuit against the complainant in a jurisdiction to which the complainant has submitted under Paragraph 3(b)(xii) of the Rules of Procedure. ....If we receive such documentation within the ten (10) business day period, we will not implement the Administrative Panel's decision, and we will take no further action, until we receive (i) evidence satisfactory to us of a resolution between the parties; (ii) evidence satisfactory to us that your lawsuit has been dismissed or withdrawn; or (iii) a copy of an order from such court dismissing your lawsuit or ordering that you do not have the right to continue to use your domain name.*

The effect of these provisions is that, by using the UDRP, a UK-based complainant will be submitting to the jurisdiction of almost certainly one and probably two courts outside of the UK. Further, if the respondent commences legal action in one of those jurisdictions within ten business days then the implementation of the UDRP decision will be suspended until such time as those court proceedings have concluded.

An incautious complainant hoping to resolve its domain name issue with a simple administrative dispute procedure could unexpectedly find itself in costly, international litigation.

Representatives should make sure that their clients are crystal clear on the jurisdiction implications of using the UDRP.

The mutual jurisdiction clause in WIPO's UDRP Model Complaint is as follows:

> ***IX. Mutual Jurisdiction***
> ***(Rules, Paragraph 3(b)(xii)).***
>
> *In accordance with Paragraph 3(b)(xii) of the Rules, the Complainant will submit, with respect to any challenges that may be made by the Respondent to a decision by the Administrative Panel to transfer or cancel the domain name(s) that is/are the subject of*

this Complaint, to the jurisdiction of the courts at [choose one of the following:]

(a) *"the location of the principal office of the concerned registrar." or*

(b) *"the location of the domain name holder's address, as shown for the registration of the domain name(s) in the concerned registrar's WhoIs database at the time of the submission of the Complaint to the Center." or*

(c) *"the location of the principal office of the concerned registrar AND the domain name holder's address, as shown for the registration of the domain name(s) in the concerned registrar's WhoIs database at the time of the submission of the Complaint to the Center."*

[A Mutual Jurisdiction election must be made for each domain name that is the subject of the Complaint.]

Complainants should make sure they have researched the possibilities (as far as the current WhoIs blackout will allow) before making their selection.

In the example of a *.com* domain registered with GoDaddy by a Russian privacy service, the initial choices of jurisdiction would be the USA (as GoDaddy is based in the USA) or Russia or both.

If once the UDRP complaint had been filed the true registrant was discovered to be a British individual, then the complainant would have the option of amending its complaint to name the true registrant as the respondent and the choices of jurisdiction would then be the USA or the UK or both.

In the reverse situation where the privacy service was UK-based and the true registrant was a Russian individual, then a UK-based complainant may prefer to keep the privacy service as the respondent and choose the jurisdiction of the UK court so as to avoid any risk of getting dragged into international litigation.

If the identity of the true registrant is known before the UDRP action is filed then potential complainants should check to see if they have a history of commencing court proceedings following UDRP actions.

For registrants which are sufficiently connected to the UK but for whom both mutual jurisdiction options are foreign jurisdictions (e.g. a *.com* domain in UK ownership but with WhoIs data listing a subsidiary or a legal representative outside of the UK), the complainant should consider bringing a case for summary judgement in the IPEC rather than a URDP action.

Although UK court action would be more expensive than the UDRP it may nevertheless be the prudent course if there is a non-negligible risk that the losing respondent might launch court proceedings in an international mutual jurisdiction.

By way of example, Yoyo.Email Limited has been an unsuccessful respondent in numerous UDRP (and URS) cases and has been willing on more than one occasion to commence related legal proceedings both in the UK[47] and internationally.[48]

7.3 The first element

The first element of the UDRP test is set out in paragraph 4(a)(i) of the UDRP Policy. It states (emphasis added):

47 *Yoyo.Email Limited v Royal Bank of Scotland Group plc & Ors [2015] EWHC 3509 (Ch)*

48 *Yoyo.Email LLC v Playinnovation Limited, Arizona District Court, Case Number: 2:2014cv01922*

> *4(a)(i) ....your domain name is identical or confusingly similar to a trademark or service mark in which the complainant has rights;*

7.3.1 Identical or confusingly similar

Complainants should not overcomplicate this issue and the threshold here is a low one representing a simple test of the complainant's standing to bring the complaint.[49]

A panel would normally find a domain name confusingly similar to the complainant's rights for purposes of UDRP standing if, on a side-by-side analysis, the rights are recognisable in the domain name. A domain which incorporates a letter string identical to the trade mark in conjunction with prefixes, suffixes or other additional matter is highly likely to be deemed confusingly similar.

In this context recognisability is now judged from both human and technological (e.g. a search engine algorithm) perspectives. This is a relatively recent development following *WIPO UDRP Case No. D2014-0778 <peopleincasinos.com>* (discussed in more detail in paragraph 7.3.1.2 below) in which the complainant's registered word mark PLEIN was not considered to be confusingly similar to the domain name. The panel took the view that the PLEIN trade mark would not be recognisable to the average Internet user as the letter string was buried within the domain and split over two words. Neither had the complainant provided any evidence of the real-world effect of the inclusion of the "plein" letter string on search engine results and had relied only on conclusory assertions to that effect. The complaint, therefore, fell at the first hurdle and the panel was not able to consider whether the respondent had registered and used the domain name in bad faith.

49 See, for example, *WIPO UDRP Case No. D2008-1986 <aubert.com>*

Phonetic and conceptual characteristics may also be taken into account and the use of homophones or conceptually similar words may lead to a finding of confusing similarity even if the letter strings might be objectively different.[50]

Panels have made it clear in numerous decisions that, although complainants must demonstrate that they own trade mark rights and show the disputed domain is "confusing similar", the UDRP is not a trade mark infringement test. References to UK or CJEU case law in relation to the global assessment of confusing similarity for the purposes of demonstrating trade mark infringement are unlikely to be helpful.

7.3.1.1 Is the TLD relevant?

The general position on this issue is that the TLD is ignored in the assessment of identity or confusing similarity. A domain name consisting of <*trademark.tld*> would be considered identical to that trade mark.[51]

In recent times the changing nature of cybersquatting activity and the release of the New gTLDs has required an updated approach in which the SLD can be considered in combination with the TLD. For example, the domain names <*tes.co*>,[52] <*b.mw*>[53] and <*swarov.ski*>[54] were considered identical to the trade marks TESCO, BMW and SWAROVSKI, respectively.

50 See, for example, *WIPO UDRP Case No. D2010-1089 <rapidpiracy.com>*

51 See, for example, *WIPO UDRP Case No. D2018-2510 <chatroulette.pro>*

52 WIPO UDRP Case DCO2013-0017

53 WIPO UDRP Case DMW2015-0001

54 WIPO UDRP Case D2016-2036

7.3.1.2 Is the content of the website relevant?

The majority of panellists take the view that the content of the website visible at the disputed domain should have no bearing on whether the domain and the rights are deemed to be confusingly similar. This is, however, an issue where panellists hold different views. The panel's refusal of the complaint in *WIPO UDRP Case No. D2014-0778 <peopleincasinos.com>* is a case in point.

The complainant in that case was the famous fashion designer Phillip Plein and, as mentioned in paragraph 7.3.1 above, the complaint failed on the basis that the complainant's rights in the PLEIN word mark were not confusingly similar to the domain name. This was despite the fact that the website visible at the domain was an exact copy of the complainant's website and it was selling allegedly counterfeit products bearing the PHILLIP PLEIN and PLEIN trade marks. It was abundantly clear that the PLEIN trade mark had been targeted by the respondent and that the domain had been registered and was being used in bad faith. The panellist's strict approach to confusing similarity mean that these other factors were not deemed sufficient for the test under the first element to be made out.

Some panellists take the view that the respondent's actions in the *<peopleincasinos.com>* case is something that the UDRP should be able to address and consider that the content of the website visible at the disputed domain should have been given more significance in the assessment of confusing similarity. Evidence showing that the complainant's website has been copied and that counterfeits of the complainant's goods are being sold via the domain creates a very strong inference that the domain registrant itself considers the rights and the domain to be sufficiently similar so as to confuse either persons or algorithms. If that is the case then the panel should have no difficulty in also finding that there is confusing similarity.

Others are of the view that if the content of the website can point *towards* a finding of confusing similarity it should also be able to point *away* from that conclusion. This might lead to the even less desirable scenario of a confusingly similar domain name being registered and used in bad faith by a cybersquatter but due to the precise nature of that use the complaint in fact fails before the bad faith assessment takes place.

Consider the example of *WIPO UDRP Case No. D2008-1267 <hairywinston.com>*. This case was not decided under the first element (it was eventually denied under the third element) but its facts make it an interesting example of how the content of the website could potentially point away from confusing similarity.

The complainant was Harry Winston Inc. a jeweller and the owner of a number of registrations consisting of or containing HARRY WINSTON. The respondent was a private individual that used the domain for her luxury pet boutique business. The domain was registered after the name of her (allegedly hairy) dog, Winston, but with the complainant's trade mark rights firmly in mind. It was intended as a play on words to convey the message of a luxury pet business but without any attempt to mislead or cause confusion.

The panel in that case had no difficulty in finding the domain to be confusingly similar to the complainant's HARRY WINSTON trade mark. If a similar set of facts were to arise in a case today it would certainly be worthwhile for the respondent to argue that the content of the website should be taken into account and that it points away from there being any confusing similarity with the complainant's rights. Even if the panellist is not sympathetic to this argument it should feed in to the considerations of legitimate interest under the second element and bad faith intent under the third element.

7.3.2 What types of rights can be relied upon?

The complainant's rights must be in a trade mark or a service mark. The rights can be either registered or unregistered but must exist at a national or regional (i.e. multi-national) level at the time the complaint is filed.

A copy of a registration certificate (along with the latest renewal certificate, if needed) or a printout from a publicly available official trade mark database is sufficient to prove the existence of a registered right.

Trade marks on sub-national registers (e.g. US state registers), pending applications, trade marks which are similar to the domain only in respect of a disclaimed part or trade marks which are registered on registers which do not require examination on inherent grounds do not automatically confer standing.

Rights are taken at face value and registrations which are, for example, subject to post registration opposition or invalidation/revocation proceedings would still confer standing.

For the purposes of the first element it does not matter in which jurisdiction the rights are registered or in respect of which goods or services. If the trade mark is registered in the respondent's home jurisdiction or is registered for goods or services the same as or similar to those visible on the respondent's website, then this will strengthen the complainant's case under the second and third elements.

Neither does it matter for the purposes of standing under the first element exactly when the rights came into being (provided it was before the complaint was filed). The complaint can proceed even if the domain name was registered many years before the complainant registered its first trade mark.

The existence of an unregistered right would need to be proven evidentially to the extent required under the relevant local law. This is (or should be!) the only part of a UDRP case where local law is relevant.

A UK-based complainant with no registered trade marks would need to rely on the UK law of passing off to give it standing under the UDRP. It would need to show that i) it has generated goodwill in a name through its use in the UK, ii) the domain is sufficiently similar to amount to a misrepresentation and iii) such misrepresentation is damaging to the goodwill in its name.

Evidence as to the existence of goodwill should ideally be approached in the normal way – i.e. a sworn statement from the rights owner setting out full details on the duration and nature of the use, the level of sales and advertising and the degree of public recognition of the mark. It is possible, however, simply to provide evidence of goodwill within the body of the complaint itself if publicly available information is sufficient and if you can do so without exceeding the word limit.

For unregistered marks which consist of descriptive terms, the complainant will also need to demonstrate that its mark has acquired distinctiveness through use. The nature of the required evidence would be the same as for demonstrating passing off but the evidential hurdle would be higher.

Since the aim of the UDRP Policy is to be global and agnostic as to the location of the parties, panels have been willing to find that complainants from civil law jurisdictions are entitled to rely on common law rights even where their home legal system does not recognise them. To do otherwise, would prejudice every complainant from a civil law jurisdiction.[55]

Panels are willing to imply the existence of an unregistered right if it is clear that the respondent's website has targeted the complainant's right. The rationale being that there must be some goodwill or secondary meaning in the complainant's right in order to make it worthwhile for the respondent to have targeted it.

The rationale for using website content to determine the existence of unregistered rights is somewhat at odds with the view that the website content cannot similarly be used to determine if those rights are confusingly similar to the domain name.

The strength of the complainant's rights can have a significant impact on the second and third elements of the UDRP test. It is worthwhile

55 See, for example, WIPO UDRP Case No. D2009-1394 <palaisstephany.com>

submitting thorough evidence, in particular, where the rights are unregistered and based on use.

Subsidiaries or exclusive licensees of the trade mark owner are considered to have standing to bring a complaint. Panels have been prepared to imply the existence of authorisation to bring enforcement action based on the underlying trade mark rights but best practice would be to include specific evidence on this point in the complaint.

Non-exclusive licensees are typically not considered to have sufficient standing and would need to file evidence of authorisation from the trade mark owner.

7.4 The second element

The second element of the UDRP test is set out in paragraph 4(a)(ii) of the UDRP Policy. It states (emphasis added):

> *4(a)(ii) ....you have no rights or legitimate interests in respect of the domain name;*

A non-exhaustive list of examples that can constitute "legitimate interests" is set out paragraph 4(c) of the UDRP Policy. These include circumstances where i) the respondent has made demonstrable preparations for use of the domain in connection with a bona fide business, ii) the respondent is commonly known by a name which corresponds to the domain name or iii) the use of the domain is legitimate non-commercial or fair use.

The material date for the assessment of the second element is the date the complaint is filed. In practice, since the time elapsed between the filing of the complaint and the evidence coming before the panel is only a few weeks at most, panellists do assess the evidence without regard to any material date.

This would, of course, be looked at more critically if an important piece of evidence dated only from after the filing of the complaint (e.g. the respondent filed a trade mark application corresponding to the domain only after it was notified of the complaint).

7.4.1 The complainant's perspective

The wording of this element requires the complainant to prove a negative in its complaint. Therefore, the complainant simply has to make out a *prima facie* case that the respondent lacks rights or legitimate interests and the burden of rebutting that *prima facie* case then shifts to the respondent.

From the complainant perspective, it is vital that the complaint states as a minimum that the respondent is not a licensee or otherwise authorised to register a domain name corresponding to its trade mark.

The complainant should put in evidence any indication that its rights have been targeted. This could be, for example, evidence that the domain has been pointed to the website of a competitor or screenshots showing that the PPC links on the respondent's website link to the complainant, its goods or to a competitor.

If the domain is being used to sell counterfeit goods, to distribute malware, as part of a scam or to sell illegal products then this should certainly be mentioned as such use will always be regarded as illegitimate.

The complainant should not take the second element too lightly, however, and should research the respondent thoroughly. As previously mentioned, the complainant is not guaranteed to be given the opportunity to file any additional evidence or arguments so it should try to anticipate whatever arguments the respondent might put forward and address these up-front.

A further reason for carrying out the research is that it might uncover evidence pointing towards the respondent's rights or legitimate interest in the domain – for example, the respondent might have its own registered trade mark corresponding to the domain. If the complainant proceeds with the complaint when it knows (or should have known) that it is doomed to fail then it is putting itself at risk of a finding of Reverse Domain Name Hijacking (this is discussed in more detail at paragraph 7.6 below).

7.4.2 The respondent's perspective

This second element is often the best chance a respondent has of defending its domain name so it is vital that a response is submitted to rebut the complainant's *prima facie* case as to lack of legitimate intent. Failure to file a response does not mean that the complainant wins by default but it certainly does make it easier for the panel to find in favour of the complainant when no arguments as to rights or legitimate interest have been raised.

If the respondent has its own trade mark corresponding to the domain then this should certainly be mentioned. Unless the complainant can show to the panel's satisfaction that the trade mark was registered primarily to frustrate the application of the UDRP, the existence of the registration will support a finding that the respondent has rights and that it has registered the domain in relation to a legitimate business.

The respondent should as a minimum explain why the domain was chosen. A credible reason that has nothing to do with the complainant (e.g. it corresponds to a school nickname or is named after a family pet) will go a long way to showing that the respondent was acting legitimately.

For domains that are in use, claims to legitimate or fair use will turn on whether the website content appears to support the claim. For example, if the website corresponds to the descriptive meaning of the domain or if it is clearly being used for a fansite or gripesite. Any use of the domain intended to cause confusion, tarnish the complainant's rights or profit from misdirected Internet traffic will be deemed illegitimate.

If it appears that the respondent does have a legitimate interest in using the domain then a clear and sufficiently prominent disclaimer can help the panel to reach a decision in favour of the respondent.[56] The inclusion of a disclaimer is not a panacea, however.

Many domains are parked and available for purchase. Panellists are now in agreement that the purchase and resale of generic domain names are of themselves entirely legitimate activities. Respondents are entitled to generate income from domains via PPC links unrelated to the complainant and which do not mislead or capitalise on the reputation and goodwill of the complainant's mark.

Respondents cannot disclaim responsibility for automatically generated PPC links that might refer to the complainant or its business. In order to benefit from the legitimate interest provision they are required to take active steps to avoid this occurrence, for example, though the use of negative keywords.

7.4.3 Freedom of Speech cases

Freedom of speech cases deserve special mention as they generate a significant amount of domain dispute activity[57] and there are tactical implications for complainants.

In general the registration of a domain name for the purposes of genuine non-commercial free speech would be considered a legitimate use of the DNS. This is provided that the domain name in question is not so similar to the complainant's rights that it amounts to an impersonation causing user confusion.

WIPO UDRP Case No. D2017-1982 <gianpaolo-dicocco.com>, <make-astrology-great-again.com>, <gianpaolo-dicocco-failed-predictions.com> & 6 others shows where the line is drawn on the issue of impersonation.

56 See for example, *WIPO UDRP Case No. D2001-0903 <okidataparts.com >*

57 *WIPO UDRP Case No. D2022-3275 <akeliusslumlord.com>*

The complainant was Paul DiCocco. He traded as an astrologer under both his own name and the pseudonym GianPaolo DiCocco. He was able to show that he had unregistered rights in both names and a US registered trade mark for MAKE ASTROLOGY GREAT AGAIN. The respondent was Curtis Lee Mickunas, also an astrologer. The parties were aware of each other and were initially cordial but subsequently had a falling out. Over the course of around 18 months the parties launched repeated reciprocal personal attacks each questioning the other's reputation and competence as an astrologer. The respondent registered the nine domain names in dispute as part of the falling out and in an effort to defend himself. The domains were either not used or resolved to non-commercial websites controlled by the respondent on which was posted content critical of the complainant's astrological-based predictions.

The panel held that the respondent did not have a legitimate interest in respect of *<gianpaolo-dicocco.com>* or *<make-astrology-great-again.com>* and six other similar domains. These domains all reproduced exactly the complainant's name and trade mark in which he had rights leading to an unacceptably high risk that an Internet user could be confused into believing that an affiliation, sponsorship or other relationship existed.

Conversely, the panel held that the respondent did have a legitimate interest in registering and using *<gianpaolo-dicocco-failed-predictions.com>*. The use was in respect of a genuine non-commercial criticism site and the domain name was such that an Internet user would immediately realise its nature and not consider it to be an official site authorised or run by the complainant.

On a tactical level, the choice of provider can have a bearing on the outcome of freedom of speech cases. This is because of the number of US panellists versus European panellists on the rota of each provider and the different approaches on freedom of speech issues in general between the US system (where freedom of speech often trumps other issues) and most European legal systems (where freedom of speech is subject to a larger degree to the rights of others).

The *WIPO UDRP Case No. D2018-1256 <ivy-lane-living.com>* shows how this can happen in practice. Both parties were from the USA and WIPO appointed a panellist also from the USA. The complainant was Courtney Cox, wife to Chris Cox (a senior figure in the National Rifle Association), and one of the owners of interior design business, Ivy Lane Living. The respondent was a political resistance group named Betsy Riot.

The respondent registered the domain name *<ivy-lane-living.com>* and used it for a website making a graphic political statement about the need for gun control in the USA. The respondent had clearly targeted the business Ivy Lane Living in order to make its political statement. That is to say that the respondent deliberately chose to not target the National Rifle Association itself but targeted instead the business of the wife of one of its officials.

National law can be considered in UDRP cases in limited situations where it is particularly germane to do so and where the nationality of both of the parties and the selected mutual jurisdiction are all the same. In this case the panellist, applying US First Amendment principles, found that the domain was being used legitimately and denied the complainant's transfer request.

There are around 125 panellists on the rota at forum and around 500 panellists on the rota at WIPO. Roughly 30-40% of the panellists for each provider are either practicing US lawyers or retired US judges. In cases where both parties are from the same jurisdiction, WIPO (and probably also Forum) deliberately appoints a panellist from that same jurisdiction. Electing WIPO as the provider practically guaranteed that a US panellist would be appointed and, whilst the quality of their decision making is not in doubt, it is inevitable that the way they perceive issues is going to be coloured by their US legal background and opens the door for US legal concepts to be applied.

At the CAC, there are currently 95 panellists of which 56 are from the EU/UK and only six are from the USA. Had the *<ivy-lane-living.com>* case been filed at the CAC the chances of it being allocated a panellist from a European legal background would have been much higher. It will, of course, never be known for certain but had the CAC been the provider US law would probably not then have factored into the decision and the case may well have been decided the other way.

The second element test is complex and subjective in that it depends in large part upon the intentions and motivations of the respondent. Even if the respondent files a response its true motivations can be difficult to ascertain in the absence of a more rigorous evidence regime, disclosure and cross-examination.

For that reason, and since failure to find legitimate interest is not fatal to the respondent's case, it is not uncommon for panellists to duck the second element test if the dispute can be more easily decided under the third element[58] (i.e. because the respondent has clearly not registered and used the domain in bad faith).

7.5 The third element

The third element of the UDRP test is set out in paragraph 4(a)(iii) of the UDRP Policy. It states (emphasis added):

> *4(a)(iii) ….your domain name has been registered* ***and*** *is being used in bad faith;*

In general, "bad faith" is found in circumstances where a respondent has taken unfair advantage of or has otherwise abused a complainant's mark.

A non-exhaustive list of examples that can constitute bad faith is set out paragraph 4(b) of the UDRP Policy. These include, situations where i) the domain was registered primarily for the purpose of selling it to a rights owner, ii) the domain was registered to block a rights owner from registering the domain itself (provided that there is a pattern of such

58 See, for example, *WIPO UDRP Case No. D2008-1267 <hairywinston.com>*

conduct), iii) the domain was registered primarily to disrupt the business of a competitor or iv) the domain is intentionally being used in manner designed to cause confusion and attract Internet traffic for commercial gain.

7.5.1 The conjunctive requirement

The requirement for both bad faith use *and* bad faith registration has generated decisions over the life of the UDRP that some consider to be unfair and inconsistent with its aims.[59] However, the line of cases that experimented with a more relaxed "unitary" approach has now been closed off and panellists are in agreement that a complainant can only succeed under the third element if the domain was registered in bad faith *and* is being used in bad faith.[60]

All the cases to date have dealt with circumstances where the registration was in good faith but the subsequent use was in bad faith. However, the conjunctive requirement would apply equally in the hypothetical example of a registration obtained in bad faith but subsequently used in good faith.

Although there is now consensus amongst UDRP panellists, the issue is still a contentious one for the Internet community and for brand owners.

The domain resale community argues strongly that, if a registrant has been prescient enough to register a domain in good faith that years down the line becomes desirable to a rights owner, then it is perfectly fair that the registrant should be able to sell that domain to the rights owner at market value rather than losing it in a UDRP action.

---

59 See, for example, the dissenting opinions in *WIPO UDRP Case No. D2010-0800 <ferrlecit.com>* and *WIPO UDRP Case No. D2013-1324 <truereligion.com>*

60 See, for example, *WIPO UDRP Case D2016-2301 <portafloor.net>*

Such a registrant should, in the meantime, be able to use its domain in any way it sees fit – even if that use monetizes the rights owner's goodwill. If the use amounted to trade mark infringement then the rights owner could still commence proceedings in the court even if a UDRP action would be doomed to failure.

Rights owners argue that the "unitary" approach is more consistent with a strict reading of the UDRP Policy[61] and it does not unfairly prejudice domain owners as they would be able to defend a UDRP complaint under the second element if they are acting legitimately.

7.5.2 Registration in bad faith

Registration in this context is understood to mean both the first registration of the domain (i.e. its creation date) and the date of any subsequent transfers in ownership. Transfer between two entities under common control will not automatically count as a new registration. The mere renewal of a domain is not regarded a new registration.

The assessment of bad faith registration is made as at the date that the respondent registered the domain. Therefore, the transfer of a domain into new ownership creates a new material date for the assessment and it is critical for complainants to determine this date accurately as it can change the entire complexion of the dispute.

The use of privacy services complicates this issue as they can mask an underlying transfer of the domain. In such circumstances, a complainant can allege that a transfer has taken place (e.g. based on evidence of a sudden change in use[62]) and it is then for the respondent to refute this. If it does not do so, panels have been willing to deem that a transfer has

61 In particular, as regards paragraph 2(d) of the UDRP Policy which imposes an ongoing obligation that the registrant "will not knowingly use the domain name in violation of any applicable laws or regulations".

62 *WIPO UDRP Case No. D2022-0910 <skill.com>*

taken place and that the use of the privacy service is a bad faith attempt to conceal the underlying registrant and the date of registration.[63]

The examples of bad faith given in paragraph 4(b) of the UDRP Policy have as their common theme a requirement that it must have been the respondent's intention at the time the domain was registered to exploit or otherwise benefit from the complainant's rights.

The jurisprudence that has developed around this limb of the third element test has followed the common theme from the Policy and complainants must demonstrate to the panel's satisfaction that the respondent both knew of and targeted its rights.

In the vast majority of cases the parties to the dispute are wholly unrelated. Requiring complainants to submit proof of what the respondent knew or did not know at the time the domain was registered would be a very high evidential hurdle. Therefore, panels have been willing to imply knowledge based on circumstantial evidence even if a respondent claims to have been unaware of the complainant's rights.

For example, if the complainant's right is well-known globally or the complainant passed through the first element test by showing strong rights in the respondent's home jurisdiction (particularly where the rights are backed up by evidence of substantial use), it will be difficult for the respondent credibly to argue that it was not aware of the complainant's rights at the time the domain name was registered.

Further, indicia of bad faith registration that panels have taken into account include:[64]

- whether the domain name is identical to or is an obvious typo of the complainant's mark;

63 *WIPO UDRP Case No. D2018-2384 <greenroads.com>; WIPO UDRP Case No. D2008-0882 <bme.com>*

64 WIPO Jurisprudential Overview 3.0, sections 3.1 and 3.2

- whether the domain name incorporates the complainant's mark along with descriptive additional matter, particularly where the additional matter is descriptive of the complainant's area of business;
- the distinctiveness of the earlier mark and the respondent's failure to provide a credible reason as to why the domain was registered;
- the historic and current content of any website visible at the domain, in particular, whether the website links to the complainant or its competitors;
- admissions made in settlement correspondence;
- threats to sell the domain to the highest bidder or to point it to content which might harm the trade mark;
- attempts to force the complainant into unwanted business arrangements or to exchange the domain for goods or services;
- the timing of the domain registration – for example if it followed a merger announcement or product launch; and
- whether the respondent has engaged in a pattern of DNS abusive behaviour or its past conduct points to previous attempts to exploit third party rights.

Panels have developed the knowledge criteria further by imposing a positive obligation on respondents who are professional domain resellers to search the freely available online trade marks registers to determine if any identical of confusingly similar rights exist.[65]

65 See, for example, *WIPO UDRP Case No. D2021-3598 <aoga.com>; WIPO UDRP Case No. D2015-1230 <bounz.com>*

Panels can be more lenient with companies or individuals regarding the extent of any searches that they should have carried out. However, the panel can find that the domain had been registered in bad faith if the respondent had been wilfully blind to the potential rights of third parties.[66]

If both the complainant and the respondent are located in the USA and the complainant owns a US federal trade mark registration, panellists have been willing to expand the scope of the respondent's knowledge further still by applying the concept of constructive notice (i.e. under US law the respondent is deemed to be aware of any and all US federal trade mark registrations).[67]

One scenario in which the respondent can quite credibly argue that it was unaware of the complainant's rights is if the domain was registered before those rights came into existence.

As discussed above in the context of the first element test, rights which have a creation date after the domain registration date do still give a complainant sufficient standing to bring the complaint. However, having standing to bring the complaint is an entirely separate issue to the assessment of registration in bad faith under the third element.

In general, it would be difficult for a complainant to show that a domain registered before the creation of its rights was registered in bad faith and the complaint would likely fail under the third element.

An exception to this general rule could be circumstances which indicate that the respondent registered the domain name specifically in anticipation of the complainant's rights coming into existence (e.g. if the respondent had insider knowledge of a corporate merger).

66 See, for example, *WIPO UDRP Case No. D2023-2100 <blendsports.com>*

67 See, for example, *WIPO UDRP Case No. D2024-5212 <dansko-clogs-women.com>; WIPO UDRP Case No. D2023-3537 <dreamcargiveaway.com>*

If the rights owner authorised the registration of the domain in the first instance (e.g. it was registered as part of a licensing or distribution arrangement) then such a registration cannot have been in bad faith. Any complaint on these facts will be doomed to fail, even if there is subsequent bad faith use, and the complainant will be at risk of a finding of Reverse Domain Name Hijacking.[68]

It is accepted by panellists that registering a domain name purely for the purposes of resale does not automatically amount to bad faith. It follows that an offer to sell a domain, whether an open offer or one made specifically to the complainant, is not in and of itself indicative of bad faith registration.[69] There would need to be something over and above this to point to the respondent's targeting of the complainant.[70]

7.5.3 Use in bad faith

Whether or not a domain has been used in bad faith is a very fact specific assessment but reaching a decision on this issue is not normally difficult – provided that the parties have supported their claims with sufficiently rigorous evidence.

At one end of the spectrum, using the domain for selling counterfeit goods, phishing, identity theft or malware distribution are clearly bad faith uses. At the other end of the spectrum, using a domain in accordance with its descriptive meaning and seeking to keep clear of the complainant's rights by employing negative keywords is a strong indicator of good faith use.

Pointing the domain at a respondent-controlled website selling competing goods or at websites of the complainant's competitors would be seen as bad faith use since this harms the reputation and distinctiveness

---

68 See, for example, *WIPO UDRP Case No. D2013-1603 <timbermate.com>*

69 See, for example, *WIPO UDRP Case No. D2016-1221 <billybobs.com>*

70 See, for example, *WIPO UDRP Case No. DCO2016-0034 <oculusrift.co>*

of the trade mark. If the complainant has evidence of actual confusion occurring in the marketplace then this should certainly be annexed to the complaint.

In this context, the presence of a disclaimer cannot remedy a respondent's bad faith. If the evidence supports a finding of bad faith then panellists are more likely to regard a disclaimer as further evidence that the respondent knew of the complainant's rights and understood that there was a risk of confusion.

Pointing the domain at the complainant's own website is also an example of bad faith use as this comes with an implied threat that any traffic reaching the complainant's website in this way can by turned on and off at the respondent's whim.

Monetizing a domain through the use of PPC links does not amount to bad faith use, provided that such links (whether automatically generated or otherwise) do not relate to the complainant, its area of business or its competitors. In order to display good faith use, a respondent is required to have taken active steps to avoid this occurrence, for example, though the use of negative keywords.

An offer to sell a domain is regarded as "use" of the domain for the purposes of this limb of the third element test.[71]

If the domain does not resolve to a website at all and neither have there been any offers for sale, panels can still find that a domain has been used in bad faith under the doctrine of passive holding.[72] Panels would be inclined to find passive holding if the complainant's mark is very distinctive or well-known, there is no plausible use of the domain that

71 See, for example, *WIPO UDRP Case No. D1999-0001 <worldwrestlingfederation.com>*

72 *WIPO UDRP Case No. D2000-0003 <telstra.org>; WIPO UDRP Case No. D2017-0246 <docmartens.xyz>*

could be good faith use and the respondent has failed to file any response or has used false contact information.[73]

The use of privacy services has become ubiquitous and no longer leads to an automatic inference of bad faith. Panels have recognised that there are many legitimate reasons why a domain registrant might want information such as its address and telephone number hidden from public view. A finding of bad faith would be supported, however, if the registrant details as disclosed to the UDRP provider by the privacy service were simply for a second privacy service.[74] Panels have held that this Russian doll scenario is a deliberate attempt to frustrate the UDRP Policy and there can be no legitimate reason why it would need to be used.

Reverse Domain Name Hijacking

Reverse Domain Name Hijacking ("RDNH") is defined in the UDRP Rules as "using the Policy in bad faith to attempt to deprive a registered domain-name holder of a domain name". The UDRP Rules elaborate, at Paragraph 15(e), that RDNH can be found where a complaint has been "brought in bad faith" or was commenced "primarily to harass the domain-name holder".

A complainant's failure to win its complaint will not lead to a finding of RDNH provided that it had an arguable case. A respondent does not have to ask for a finding or RDNH and the panel will consider this automatically in the event that the complaint is unsuccessful.

---

73 *WIPO UDRP Case No. D2025-1631 <borbonecaffe.com>;* WIPO Jurisprudential Overview 3.0, section 3.3

74 *WIPO UDRP Case No. D2025-2924 <lincolnelectriics.com>; WIPO UDRP Case No. D2011-1857 <mycitylego.com>*

Factors which may prompt a panel to declare that a complaint was an abuse of the administrative proceeding and amounted to RDNH include:[75]

i. the complainant knew that the complaint could not succeed (for example, if it acquired its rights long after the disputed domain was registered) or it ought to have known the complaint could not succeed (for example, if the domain was clearly being used legitimately);

ii. the complainant unreasonably ignored established Policy precedent;

iii. the complainant attempted to mislead the panel (for example, by the submission of false or intentionally incomplete evidence);[76]

iv. failure to disclose that a case is a UDRP refiling;

v. basing the complaint only on conclusory allegations which are unsupported by any evidence at all.[77]

There is no sanction for a complainant that has been found guilty of RDNH. However, it is embarrassing and generates bad publicity.

Some national courts will award punitive damages to a domain registrant if the equivalent of RDNH is deemed to have occurred under local law. A finding of RDNH, therefore, may prompt a respondent to commence related court action in a mutual jurisdiction under paragraph 4(k) of the Policy.

Every finding of RDNH undermines the credibility of UDRP itself as it shows that not only are complainants not using the Policy in the intended

---

75 WIPO Jurisprudential Overview 3.0, section 4.16

76 See, for example, *WIPO UDRP Case No. D2025-2879 <royalportrush.com>*

77 See, for example, *WIPO UDRP Case No. D2024-4861 <hive-pt.com>*

way (i.e. to address only obvious cases of cybersquatting) but also that complainants are actively abusing the proceedings.

7.7 Conclusion

The number of UDRP cases filed shows that it is popular with complainants and that it is functioning, as its creators intended, as a cost effective, reliable and cross-border means for resolving domain name disputes outside of court.

Its requirements are generally now settled and well understood, yet its flexibility has allowed it to evolve over the years and keep pace with new forms of DNS abuse that were never envisaged when the Policy was written.

Potential complainants should remember that the UDRP is not, and does not aim to be, a panacea for all domain name disputes. It is there only to deal with the most obvious cases of cybersquatting and other bad faith behaviour. The ownership of a trade mark corresponding to a domain name does not automatically confer the right to ownership of that domain name.

Alongside its preparation for the second phase of the new gTLD program, ICANN is carrying out a review of all of the various Rights Protection Mechanisms. The review encompasses the UDRP[78] and all of the new mechanisms created during the first round of mew gTLDs (e.g. the TMCH and the URS). The initial report of the UDRP review project team was published in April 2025.[79]

The project team have been able to reach a unanimous decision on many of the proposed changes but some of the more contentious issues are still

78 https://www.wipo.int/amc/en/domains/resources/wipo-icaudrpreview.html

79 https://www.wipo.int/export/sites/www/amc/en/docs/wipoicareportapril2025.pdf

slated for further discussion. Agreement has been reached on the recommendations below:

- Rejection of the proposal that the loser pays and that there should be costs and damages awarded.

- There should be a fixed length of time for complainants to pay any additional required filing fees in three-member panel cases

- ICANN should boost its role in ensuring registrar's compliance with their UDRP duties

- ICANN should provide UDRP-related information and training for registrars

- The rules on withdrawal of UDRP complaints should be standardised across all providers

- If necessary to clarify, the registrant's registration data be provided to both parties and the panel by the Provider.

- Dissenting panellists should be identified in all decisions

- ICANN should contribute a small subsidy drawn from registration fees towards, for example, lowering complaint filing fees, education and training, panel remuneration, and developing UDRP guidance material

- The creation and publication of educational material for use by all parties

- Mandatory mediation should not be adopted but mediation should be offered to those that want it

- A statute of limitation period should not be adopted but delay can be factored into panellist's decisions

- The UDRP should remain focussed only on trade mark-based cybersquatting cases

- Best practices applicable to redaction of party names by panellists should be further shared and published

- Registrars should also provide notice to respondents when a UDRP action has been filed.

Agreement has not yet been reached on the issues below:

- Whether appeals should be possible

- Whether the conjunctive requirement should be removed in limited scenarios (e.g. a licensee/former employee registering in good faith but subsequently using in bad faith)

- There should be an improved and uniform manner of treating supplemental filings,

- There should be an expedited or summary procedure

- "True cancellation" should be a remedy so that the domain can never again be registered by any other party

- Panellists should have performance reviews and continuing education

- Whether existing case law should be codified and made binding across all Providers

- Clarification of the application of the UDRP to free speech issues to create consistency across providers

- Update the decision format to improve readability and uniformity

Phase 2 of the review process is expected to be lengthy. The final results of the review are expected in 2028/2029.

CHAPTER EIGHT

THE UNIFORM RAPID SUSPENSION SYSTEM ("URS")

The URS was created as part of the first New gTLD program following a recommendation that there was a need for a faster version of the UDRP to tackle the most obvious cases of online trade mark infringement. It was not designed as a replacement to the UDRP but rather as a complementary mechanism.

A review of the URS was carried out in 2024 and an updated version came into in force on 21 August 2025.

8.1 Differences to the UDRP

The URS is based on the UDRP and it has very similar characteristics. There are, however, some important differences of which users should be aware.

The URS is applicable to domain name registrations in all of the New gTLDs, the legacy gTLDs *.asia*, *.biz*, *.cat*, *.info*, *.jobs*, *.mobi*, *.museum*, *.org*, *.pro*, *.tel*, *.travel* and *.xxx* and the *.pw* ccTLD. This means that URS cases cannot be brought against domains registered in the *.com* and *.net* legacy gTLDs which are the largest TLDs by some considerable margin.

Forum, the Asian Domain Name Dispute Resolution Centre ("ADNDRC") and MFSD[80] are the only providers of URS services. WIPO is a notable absentee from this list and it has been critical of the

80 The MFSD IP Dispute Resolution Center is an Italian ADR provider. It also provides the .it domain dispute resolution service (https://urs.mfsd.it)

URS since before its launch, suggesting that the process is trying to do "too much for too little".[81]

The URS is a useful addition to the armoury of a potential complainant but it has not proven to be popular and it is used far less than the UDRP. In 2024 there were roughly 6,100 UDRP complaints filed at WIPO and roughly 2,500 filed at Forum. In the same time period there were only 170 URS cases decided by Forum, 40 cases decided by MFSD and 26 cases decided by ADNDRC.

One possible explanation for its underutilisation may be that the URS got off to a somewhat rocky start with a number of early users being caught out by the differences to the UDRP and eventually losing their complaints.[82]

Further, although the URS is significantly quicker than the UDRP (taking roughly 21 days to complete) this may still be too slow for those extremely urgent, clear-cut cases it is designed to address. If the domain registrant's bad faith is so apparent (e.g. if the domain is being used for a phishing scam) then seeking a registrar takedown may be a more appropriate course.

In order to succeed in a URS case a complainant must meet the three elements of a standard UDRP case[83] but must prove their claims with clear and convincing[84] evidence. The burden of proof standard under the UDRP is that claims must be proven on the "balance of probabilities". In addition, the complainant's rights must take the form of a registered

81 URS 2.0? WIPO Discussion Contribution, David Roache-Turner, Toronto, October 2012; https://www.wipo.int/export/sites/www/amc/en/docs/urs2.0toronto2012.pdf

82 See, for example, *Forum Case FA1408001575592 <eharmony.email>*

83 URS Procedure, paragraph 8.1

84 URS Procedure, paragraph 8.2

trade mark for an unstylised word that is proven to be in use[85] or a trade mark verified by court proceedings or protected by a statute or treaty.

There must also be no genuine issue of material fact[86] and there must be no non-infringing use or fair use of the relevant trade mark.[87]

The requirement that the registrant's use cannot be non-infringing use means that cases suitable for determination under the URS sit in the relatively narrow overlap of situations that amount to both clear trade mark infringement and actionable bad faith under the UDRP.

If a complainant succeeds in a URS case the offending domain is suspended[88] for the balance of its registration period. The domain will simply point to a web page providing information about the URS. At the end of the registration period the domain will go back into general circulation for lack of renewal. If the complainant chooses to, it can pay for the renewal of the domain (and thus continue the suspension) for an extra year.

The URS came into some early criticism as its remedy of suspension was considered to be too weak. However, for rights holders who are increasingly trying to avoid accumulating large portfolios of domains which have no commercial use, the remedy of suspension may appear more attractive than transfer or cancellation. The URS suspension remedy is in a similar vein to domain blocking services in that it allows rights owners to balance the costs of brand protection with portfolio maintenance.

---

85 A validated TMCH record will suffice for this purpose – URS Procedure, paragraph 8.1.2.1

86 URS Procedure, paragraph 8.3

87 URS Procedure, paragraph 8.4

88 URS Procedure, paragraph 10

Complainants can use the URS without prejudice to any subsequent UDRP action or court proceedings[89] and for this reason it is most effective when used similarly to a preliminary injunction. That is to say that a complainant can use the URS to suspend the domain as a quick first step and then use the UDRP at its leisure to seek transfer of the domain.[90]

Significantly, it is possible under the URS for complainants to be sanctioned for abuse of the URS proceeding.[91] Two forms of abusive behaviour are envisaged and findings of either "abusive complaint" or "deliberate material falsehood" are possible.

A URS examiner may find that a complaint is abusive if it was presented for an improper purpose[92] (such as to harass, delay or cause increased costs to the respondent) or if the claims were not warranted by law or the URS standards or if no supporting evidence was filed.[93]

A URS examiner may find that complaint contained a deliberate material falsehood if an assertion of fact was made which was known to be untrue and which, had it been true, would have had an impact on the outcome on the URS proceeding.[94]

Complainants in receipt of two findings of abusive complaint or one finding of material falsehood will be banned from using the URS for one

89 URS Procedure, paragraph 13

90 See for example, *Yves Saint Laurent v. Khita Kongsansatien, NAF Claim No. 1565626* – a successful URS case and *Yves Saint Laurent v. Khita Kongsansatien, WIPO UDRP Case No. D2016-0496 <saintlaurent.club> and <ysl.club>* – a successful UDRP case

91 URS Procedure, paragraph 11

92 URS Procedure, paragraph 11.2.1

93 URS Procedure, paragraph 11.2.2

94 URS Procedure, paragraph 11.3

year. If a complainant is found guilty of material falsehood on two occasions then it will be permanently banned from using the URS.[95]

The URS does not incorporate any penalty for a registrant's abuse of process or repeated bad faith behaviour.

8.2 Procedure

The basic procedure[96] of the URS is as follows:

1. The complaint is filed with an ICANN-accredited provider chosen by the complainant (limited to 500 words excluding annexes) and the filing fee must be paid within one day
2. Formalities examination – if any filing deficiencies are found the complaint is dismissed without prejudice (within two business days)
3. The provider immediately notifies the appropriate registrar that a URS case has been filed and the domain is then "locked" so that it cannot be transferred into new ownership (within one day)
4. The respondent is notified (within one day)
5. The respondent files its response (limited to 2,500 words excluding annexes). The response/re-examination fee, if any, must be paid within one day. Failure to file a response will not result in default judgement in favour of the complainant (within 14 days – extendible up to seven days if there is a good faith basis for doing so)

---

95 URS Procedure, paragraph 11.4 and 11.5

96 URS Rules, paragraphs 3 and 5; URS Procedure, paragraph 1, 3, 4, 5, 6, 9 and 12; http://newgtlds.icann.org/en/applicants/urs/rules-04mar13-en.pdf; http://newgtlds.icann.org/en/applicants/urs/procedure-01mar13-en.pdf

6. Immediate appointment of an Examiner

7. Issuance of the Examiner's decision (within three business days)

8. The registrar is immediately notified of decision and domain is either suspended or unlocked

9. If default decision was issued (i.e. no response was filed) then the respondent can file a late response within 6 months and ask for a *de novo* review

    a. A late filed response is free for first 30 days

    b. A re-examination fee of USD 200 is payable thereafter (this fee is as specified in Forum's Supplemental Rules)

    c. The deadline for filing a late response is extendable by a further 6 months upon request and payment of USD 100 (this fee is as specified in Forum's Supplemental Rules)

10. *De novo* appeal by either party is possible with the costs payable by appellant (within 14 days)

Each provider has its own Supplemental Rules regarding specific procedural issues (e.g. the timing of payment of the appropriate fees, requesting extensions of time and suspensions to allow settlement negotiations).

The ability of examiners to request the submission of additional evidence and arguments is expressly ruled out97 in order to keep the procedure as streamlined as possible.

In a further effort to reduce complexity, the URS Procedure states that all complaints must be filed in English and will be translated by the provider. The registrant will be notified of the complaint both in English

97 URS Rules, paragraph 10

and in the predominant language of its country.[98] The response can be either in English or in the second language and the appointed examiner will be fluent in both languages. The language of the decision itself can be either English or the second language and will be decided at the examiner's discretion.[99]

8.3 Costs

The URS is significantly cheaper than the UDRP. The fee varies by provider but the filing fee for a decision against a single domain name will not be above USD 375.

There are no costs awards payable to either party but a successful complainant will be repaid a proportion of the filing by the respondent if 15 or more domains were in issue and the respondent has participated in the proceedings.

If a losing URS complainant at Forum commences within 30 days a UDRP action also at Forum against the same respondent and in respect of the same domain name a portion of the filing fee will be refunded.

Detailed costs breakdowns for Forum and MSFD are set out in the tables below.

98 URS Procedure, paragraph 4.2

99 URS Rules, paragraph 9

Forum costs breakdown[100]

Fee type	Paid by	Amount (USD)		Refundable?
Filing fee	Complainant	Number of Domains	Fee	No
		1-14	375	
		15-30	400	
		31-50	500	
		> 51	To be agreed with Forum on a case-by-case basis	
Response fee	Respondent	Number of Domains	Fee	Yes – to successful party
		15-50	400	
		51-100	450	
		> 101	500	
Re-examination fee (more than 30 days late)	Respondent	200		No
Re-examination extension fee	Respondent	100		No
Appeal (no new material)	Appellant	Panel size	Fee	No
		1	300	
		3	950	
Appeal (new material)	Appellant	Panel size	Fee	No
		1	450	
		3	1300	

100 Forum URS Supplemental Rules, paragraph 18

Appeal to UDRP	Appellant (now UDRP complainant)	Forum will credit half of the filing fee paid in a Forum-administered URS case to the filing of a Forum-administered UDRP case for the same domain names, by the same Complainant, and between the same Parties, if the Appeal to the UDRP is filed within 30 Calendar Days.

MFSD costs breakdown

Examination and Re-examination

- EUR 550 per complaint for 1 disputed domain
- EUR 100 for each additional disputed domain in the same complaint

Appeal

- EUR 1100 per complaint for 1 disputed domain
- EUR 100 for each additional disputed domain in the same appeal

8.4 Conclusion

The URS was designed to fill a niche that in practice is turning out to be extremely narrow. This is impacting on the number of cases coming through the system with the knock-on effect that many complainants are still yet to become fully comfortable with the system.

The URS comes into its own when it is used as a form of preliminary injunction prior to a UDRP action. However, this will probably only help in a relatively narrow set of circumstances.

For extremely urgent cases of obvious bad faith use (e.g. if the domain is being used for fraud or malware distribution) the URS is still too slow and a registrar take down may be a more appropriate course of action.

For less urgent cases complainants can use the UDRP in the first instance so as to take transfer of the domain in a single proceeding.

The remedy of suspension is perhaps helpful for complainants that are trying to avoid their domain portfolios becoming bloated but for the type of slam-dunk case envisaged by the Policy, most complainants would likely want to ensure that that domain name never made it back into general availability.

CHAPTER NINE

NOMINET DRS

For over 29 years Nominet has been the registry for the *.uk* ccTLD. It is the only provider of *.uk* domain name dispute resolution services.

Nominet's Dispute Resolution Service ("DRS") was launched in 2001, only two years after the UDRP, and it has grown and matured alongside the UDRP over the years. Accordingly, although the DRS has some important differences to the UDRP, many of its concepts and the way it approaches the assessment of rights and respondent behaviour will be familiar to UDRP complainants. This section reviews the DRS from a comparative standpoint and picks out for detailed discussion only those areas which have important differences to the UDRP.

It should be noted, however, that the DRS and the UDRP are distinct systems and the citing of UDRP precedent in a DRS case is unlikely to be helpful.

The *.uk* ccTLD is the third[101] largest ccTLD by number of reported domain names and contains approximately 10 million registrations. Nominet's statistics show that roughly 13,000 complaints have been filed since the DRS was created giving a dispute rate of roughly 0.13% which is approximately triple the equivalent dispute rate under the UDRP.[102]

In 2024, 45% of DRS complaints resulted in transfer. 14% being voluntary transfers following settlement. This transfer rate is much lower than the corresponding statistic under the UDRP despite the fact that

101 Behind *.cn* and *.de*. The *.tk* ccTLD (representing Tokelau) is technically third in the list and pushes *.uk* down into fourth place but it has been discounted as it is a free registry open to all and, thus, is not operating as a standard ccTLD.

102 Crudely calculated to be 0.04% in Chapter 7 above.

DRS cases should also be self-selecting for a successful outcome for complainants and the DRS test is less restrictive than the three elements of the UDRP.

The higher dispute rate and the lower transfer rate are both likely to stem from the fact that complaints are free to file and many complainants do not seek professional assistance or heed Nominet's warnings that complaints which appear overly brief or unsupported by evidence might be deficient. A large number of the complaints that fail do so because of unclear pleadings supported by insufficient or poor evidence or even, surprisingly commonly, no evidence at all.

The basic DRS test is set out at paragraph 2 of the DRS Policy. It states as follows:

> *2 Disputes to which the DRS applies*
>
> *2.1 A Respondent must submit to proceedings under the DRS if a Complainant asserts to us, according to the Policy, that:*
>
> *2.1.1 The Complainant has Rights in respect of a name or mark which is identical or similar to the Domain Name; and*
>
> *2.1.2 The Domain Name, in the hands of the Respondent, is an Abusive Registration.*
>
> *2.2 The Complainant is required to prove to the Expert that both elements are present on the balance of probabilities.*

The basic procedure[103] of the DRS is as follows:

1. Complaint filed online (limited to 5,000 words excluding annexes) – the complaint can name more than one complainant

103 DRS Policy, paragraphs 4, 6, 7, 9, 10, 12, 13, 18, 19 and 20

2. Formalities examination – if any filing deficiencies are found the complaint is dismissed without prejudice (within two business days)

3. The respondent is notified (within three days)

4. The respondent files its response online (limited to 5000 words excluding annexes) (within 15 days). Failure to file a response will not result in default judgement in favour of the complainant

5. The complainant is notified of the response (within three days)

6. The complainant files its reply online (limited to 2,000 words excluding annexes) (within five days)

7. Mediation commences (within three days) only if the respondent has filed a response and with a maximum length of ten days

8. Complainant pays the required fee for either a full or summary decision (within ten days). Summary decisions are only possible if the respondent has not submitted a response. Failure to pay the fee results in the complaint being deemed withdrawn without prejudice. The respondent can choose to pay for a full decision (within ten further days) if it has submitted a response and taken part in the mediation

9. Expert appointed on a taxi rank system after payment of fee (within five days)

10. Decision issued (within 15 days)

11. Decision communicated to the parties and published on Nominet's website (within three days)

12. Decision implemented (within ten days) unless an intention to appeal is communicated to Nominet

13. Appeal by either party is possible with the costs payable by appellant (within 15 days)

The DRS Policy states at paragraph 26 that domain transfers during the pendency of a DRS or court proceeding and for ten days thereafter are not permitted, unless it is to the complainant as part of an amicable settlement and approved by Nominet. Nominet reserves the right to reverse any unpermitted transfer.

Importantly, the complainant has the guaranteed opportunity to reply to any response that the respondent might file. This means that complainants do not have to anticipate a respondent's arguments and counter them at the time of filing the complaint. However, any reply evidence must be strictly limited to addressing the points raised in the response so complainants should still be sure to set out their own case as thoroughly as possible at the first opportunity.

Nominet's statistics show the average time to reach a decision is 60 days for a summary decision (i.e. if no response is filed) and 78 days for full decision.

All DRS cases are heard by a single expert at first instance. Appeals are heard by a panel of three experts. Of the four appeals heard in 2024, three resulted in the original decision being overturned.

The language of the dispute is always to be English[104] and the parties must submit to the exclusive jurisdiction of the English courts and any proceedings are to be governed by English law.[105]

Mann J in his judgment of *Toth v Emirates,*[106] struck out a request from Mr Toth (the losing respondent in *DRS Appeal Case No. 8634 <emirates.co.uk>*) for the court to issue a declaration that the domain name in dispute was not an Abusive Registration within the meaning of the DRS Policy. In doing so, Mann J made it clear that the court would

104 DRS Policy, paragraph 3.3

105 DRS Policy, paragraph 4.3.9

106 *[2012] EWHC 517 (Ch), at paragraphs 48 & 65*

not act as a further instance of appeal and that the question of whether a domain name is an abusive registration is one for the expert only.

DRS costs

Action	**Fee (£) (ex. VAT)**
Complaint filing fee	-
Mediation fee	-
Expert decision (summary)	200
Expert decision (full)	750
Appeal filing fee	3000

There is no fee for the filing of the complaint itself or for the mediation. Neither is there any scaling of the fees for complaints involving multiple domain names.

The decision and appeal fees are flat rates and no additional fees are payable if experts call for additional evidence or if any extensions of time are sought.

9.1 Contents of the complaint and the response

Nominet produces and maintains an overview of expert's decisions[107] on the key DRS requirements as well as example complaint forms[108] and

107 https://media.nominet.uk/wp-content/uploads/2018/09/24124932/expert-overview.pdf

108 https://www.nominet.uk/wp-content/uploads/2025/03/Example-complaint-form.pdf

response forms.[109] These should without a doubt be the starting points for any party filing a complaint or a response.

Whilst the experts are not strictly bound by previous decisions, they will try to be consistent with them – particularly as regards appeal panel decisions. So, similarly to the position under the UDRP, the most convincing arguments will be based on the consensus views expressed in the Expert's Overview document.

If the Expert's Overview does not support a complainant's case, it should argue from first principles why in the particular circumstances in question the expert should depart from the consensus view and hold in its favour. Simply relying on the one precedent that might support its position is unlikely to get a complainant over the wining line.

There have been four different iterations of the DRS Policy and Procedure since its creation. The current version consolidates the Policy and Procedure into a single new Policy[110] and it has been applicable to *.uk* disputes filed on or after 1st October 2016.

The various iterations of the DRS Policy have remained largely unchanged in substantive terms and expert decisions issued under previous versions will still be persuasive under the current version.

Paragraph 2.2 of the DRS Policy states that the standard of proof is to be "on the balance of probabilities". In circumstances where a complainant makes a serious allegation of wrongdoing against the respondent the expert will expect to see stronger evidence to support such allegations.[111] This reflects the general position under English law that serious wrongdoing is unusual and less likely to occur it therefore takes

---

109 https://nominet.uk/wp-content/uploads/2025/03/Example_Response_Form_v5.pdf

110 https://media.nominet.uk/wp-content/uploads/2017/10/17150434/final-proposed-DRS-policy.pdf

111 *DRS Case No. 07599 <chiesi.co.uk>*

proportionately stronger evidence to prove a serious allegation on the balance of probabilities.

9.2 The first element

The first element of the test is set out in paragraph 2.1.1 of the DRS Policy. It states (emphasis added):

> *2.1.1 .... The Complainant has Rights in respect of a name or mark which is identical or similar to the Domain Name;*

The purpose of the first element test is simply to make a complainant demonstrate that it has a *bona fide* basis for making the complaint. Accordingly, the threshold here is a low one and the question falls to be considered at the time of filing the complaint.

9.2.1 What types of rights can be relied upon?

This aspect of the first element test includes a number of significant differences to the UDRP.

The first element test recognises rights in respect of a "name or mark" and is not limited to trade mark or service mark rights. The rights must be enforceable[112] under English law or otherwise and paragraph 5.1.5 of the DRS Policy specifically recognises that contractual relationships between the parties might give rise to enforceable rights.[113]

A mere company name registration (i.e. with no accompanying use in trade) in and of itself does not give rise to enforceable rights. However, experts have been willing to find that an individual may have enforceable rights in a personal name (even though there has been no accompanying

112 DRS Policy, paragraph 1

113 See by way of example *DRS Case No. 11348 <tmgtelecom.co.uk>*

use in trade) on the basis of the Human Rights Act 1998 and the Data Protection Act 1998.[114]

9.2.2 Identical or similar

The creators of the DRS Policy were well aware of the troubles early UDRP complainants encountered in showing that they owned "confusingly similar" rights. The DRS Policy, therefore, deliberately omitted this requirement and the rights need only be similar to the disputed domain name in order for the low threshold of the first element to be met.

Similarity itself is assessed on the familiar principles of the respective visual, phonetic and conceptual characteristics and whether or not the right is recognisable in the domain. DRS precedent has not as yet had to tackle the issue of whether similarity in this context includes the use of letter strings likely to be picked up by computer algorithms. An expert facing this question would likely give close consideration to the precedent that has arisen under the UDRP.

9.3 The second element

The second element of the test is set out in paragraph 2.1.2 of the DRS Policy. It states (emphasis added):

> ***2.1.2*** *.... The Domain Name, in the hands of the Respondent, is an Abusive Registration;*

114 *DRS Case No. 12276 <hvidbro-mitchell.co.uk>*

9.3.1 Abusive Registration

The concept of Abusive Registration is defined at paragraph 1 of the DRS Policy as a domain name which either (emphasis added):

> *(i) was registered or otherwise acquired in a manner which, at the time when the registration or acquisition took place, took unfair advantage of or was unfairly detrimental to the Complainant's Rights; or*
>
> *(ii) is being or has been used in a manner which has taken unfair advantage of or has been unfairly detrimental to the Complainant's Rights.*

Whilst the two elements of the test at paragraph 2 of the DRS Policy are cumulative, the concept of Abusive Registration is based around unfair advantage/detriment *either* at the time of registration of the domain *or* at any point during its subsequent use.

This of course means that there is no conjunctive requirement under the DRS and a complainant can succeed versus a domain name which predates its rights if the subsequent use of the domain renders it an Abusive Registration. This is the case even if the unfair use only took place for a short period of time and had ceased by the time the complaint was brought.

The definition of Abusive Registration is all-encompassing and gives broad discretion to the DRS experts.

The DRS Policy sets out at paragraph 5.1 a non-exhaustive list of factors which can support a claim that the disputed domain is an Abusive Registration. These include evidence that:

1. The domain was registered primarily to sell it to the complainant or a competitor for valuable consideration in excess of the respondent's out-of-pocket expenses

2. The domain was registered primarily to block the complainant or unfairly disrupt its business

3. Use or threatened use causing or likely to cause confusion with the complainant

4. The respondent has engaged in a pattern of cybersquatting behaviour

5. The respondent provided false contact details

6. The domain was registered due to relationship between the parties and the complainant has been using it exclusively and has paid for the registration/renewal

7. The domain is an exact match to a mark with a reputation and the respondent has no reasonable justification for having registered the domain

Many of these factors will be familiar to UDRP complainants but there are two points of noticeable difference.

Firstly, the Policy specifically allows for the situation where a domain was registered in good faith on behalf of the complainant but has subsequently become an Abusive Registration. This situation commonly arises where an IT services supplier, licensor or distributor has registered a domain on behalf of a rights holder but the parties subsequently fall out and rights owner seeks to recover the domain.

Secondly, threatened use alone can be sufficient to render a domain name Abusive. The effect of this is that a respondent could lose its domain to a complainant even if it had only made perfectly legitimate use of the domain and the registration of the domain predated the creation of the complainant's rights. The risk to respondents is particularly high if they make in settlement negotiations threats to change to a confusing use in a misguided attempt to bump up any sale price.

If the expert is convinced that the respondent had knowledge of the complainant's rights and that it intended to target those rights then

Abusive Registration is likely to be found. The doctrine of constructive knowledge has been applied in the context of bulk transfers of domains as due diligence should have carried out before any purchase completed.

Experts' views do differ on whether a domain can be held to be an Abusive Registration regardless of the respondent's motives. The majority of experts consider that use of a domain name which amounts to trade mark infringement or passing off would not automatically render it Abusive and that reprehensible behaviour on the part of the respondent is required. This is particularly the case where the registration of the domain predates the creation of the complainant's rights.

Paragraph 5.3 of the Policy states that there shall be a rebuttable presumption of Abusive Registration if the respondent has three or more DRS losses in the 2 years preceding the filing of the complaint. This three strikes rule has come under repeated fire from the domain resale community but it does serve the useful function of giving impetus to settlement negotiations and assisting complainants against persistent cybersquatters.

The DRS Policy sets out at paragraph 8 a non-exhaustive list of factors which can support a claim that the disputed domain is not an Abusive Registration. These include evidence that:

1. Before being aware of the complainant's cause for complaint the respondent has made genuine use of (or can demonstrate preparations to use) the domain, been commonly known by the name or connected with a mark which is identical or similar to the domain

2. The domain is generic or descriptive and the respondent's use is fair

Fair use in this context encompasses use for a fansite or gripesite and the Policy also explicitly states that trading in domain names for profit and the sale of traffic (i.e. through the use of PPC links) are not in themselves objectionable activities.[115]

9.4 Reverse Domain Name Hijacking

RDNH is broadly defined in paragraph 1 of the DRS policy as "using the DRS in bad faith in an attempt to deprive a Respondent of a Domain Name". The Expert's Overview does not elaborate on what factors might give grounds for an RDNH finding.

The definition closely reflects the corresponding wording under the UDRP and DRS experts have broadly followed the considerations as to complainant bad faith developed in that context – albeit that experts have been clear to state that the systems are different and that no reliance as such has been placed on the UDRP jurisprudence.[116]

The fact that, at the time of writing, there have only ever been 19 findings of RDNH in over 16,000 decided cases may be a consequence of the fact that complainants face a two-year ban from using the DRS if found guilty of RDNH on three separate occasions within a two-year period.

9.5 Conclusion

Nominet's DRS is an award-winning domain name dispute procedure and it is very user-friendly for both complainants and respondents.

The free meditation service is a valuable feature that frequently results in amicable settlements.

The broad discretion given to experts in finding Abusive Registration means that neither complainants nor respondents have to worry

115 DRS Policy, paragraphs 8.4 and 8.5

116 *DRS Appeal Case No. D00018931, <dignity.co.uk>* and *DRS Case No. D00020783, <pusher.co.uk>*

particularly about getting tripped up by technical legal points. All they have to do is clearly state their case and leave it up to the expert to make an adjudication.

CHAPTER TEN

EUR*ID* ADR

The *.eu* ccTLD was implemented by the adoption of European Parliament and Council Regulation (Regulation (EC) No 733/2002). It was added to the root zone of the DNS in May 2005.

The sunrise period for the new *.eu* ccTLD commenced in December 2005. The *.ею* ccTLD (the Cyrillic script equivalent to *.eu*) was launched in June 2016 and the *.ευ* ccTLD (the Greek script equivalent to *.eu*) was launched in 14 November 2019. As at Q1 of 2025 the *.eu*, *.ею* and *.ευ* ccTLDs contained a combined total of approximately 3.7 million domains.

The oversight of the *.eu*, *.ею* and *.ευ* ccTLDs (hereinafter collectively referred to as the *.eu* ccTLDs) was initially governed by EU Regulations but in October 2022 this was changed to a contractual model to give EUR*id* more flexibility and adaptability in how it provides its services as registry operator.[117] The current contact runs until October 2027 with an option to extend until October 2032.

The legal bases for the *.eu* alternative dispute resolution ("ADR") proceeding and procedure are set out in Regulation (EU) 2019/517, at Article 11 of Commission Implementing Regulation (EU) 2020/857 ("the Regulation"), and the ADR Rules[118] as published on EUR*id*'s website.

---

117 https://ec.europa.eu/digital-single-market/en/news/agreement-new-rules-functioning-eu-top-level-domain; https://eurid.eu/en/news/eurid-signs-the-new-service-concession-contract-wi/

118 https://cdn.eurid.eu/assets/adr_rules-2.pdf

The Regulation and the ADR Rules were drafted with the UDRP firmly in mind and many of its concepts and wording are the same. They do contain, however, some deliberate and important departures from the UDRP Policy and Rules. This chapter reviews the ADR from a comparative standpoint and picks out for detailed discussion only those areas which have important differences to the UDRP.

The basic ADR test is set out in Article 21(1) of the Regulation and at paragraph B(11)(d)(1) of the ADR Rules. It states as follows:

> ***B(11) Basis for Decision***
>
> *(d) The Panel shall issue a decision granting the remedies requested under the Procedural Rules in the event that the Complainant proves*
>
> *(1) in ADR Proceedings where the Respondent is the holder of a .eu domain name registration in respect of which the Complaint was initiated, that:*
>
> > *(i) The domain name is identical or confusingly similar to a name in respect of which a right is recognized or established by the national law of a Member State and/or European Union law and; either*
> >
> > *(ii) The domain name has been registered by the Respondent without rights or legitimate interest in the name; or*
> >
> > *(iii) The domain name has been registered or is being used in bad faith.*

The three elements are not cumulative and a complaint will succeed if the first element and either the second or the third element is proven. There is no conjunctive requirement within the third element test.

The required standard of proof is not specifically addressed in the Regulation or the ADR Rules but the strong consensus view amongst panellists is that complainants must make out their claims on the balance of probabilities.

A successful complainant is entitled either to cancellation of the disputed domain or to take transfer of it. The transfer remedy is only available to complainants which meet the eligibility criteria[119] set out below for holding a *.eu* domain.

3 Eligibility criteria *Registration of one or more domain names under the .eu TLD can be requested by any of the following:*		
	(a)	*a Union citizen, independently of their place of residence;*
	(b)	*a natural person who is not a Union citizen and who is a resident of a Member State;*
	(c)	*an undertaking that is established in the Union; and*
	(d)	*an organisation that is established in the Union without prejudice to the application of national law.*

In this context the "*Union*" means the EU member states as well as Iceland, Norway and Liechtenstein.

The basic procedure[120] of the ADR is as follows:

1. Complaint filed online with an EUR*id*-accredited provider chosen by the complainant and pays the required fee (within ten days)

2. Formalities examination (and any filing deficiencies remedied within seven days)

119 Article 3 of Regulation (2019/517)

120 ADR Rules, paragraphs A6, B1, B2, B3, B12 and B13

3. The provider notifies the appropriate registrar that an ADR case has been filed and the domain is then "locked" so that it cannot be transferred into new ownership (within five days)

4. The respondent is notified (within five working days)

5. The respondent files its response online (within 30 working days). Any deficiencies are to be remedied within seven days. Failure to file a response will not result in default judgement in favour of the complainant

6. Appointment of the panel of one or three persons in accordance with the specific provider's internal procedures

7. Issuance of the panel's decision (within one month)

8. Notification of decision (within three working days)

9. Implementation of the panel's decision by Registrar (within 30 days – subject to notification of commencement of court proceedings).

The complaint and any response are limited to 5000 words by the Supplemental Rules of the providers.

The CAC's statistics show the average time to reach a decision is 8-12 weeks.

The language of the ADR proceedings must be one of the official EU languages and, unless otherwise agreed, will be the language of the domain registration agreement. If a complainant wishes the proceedings to take place in a different language, it must make a written request and pay the required fee. The adjudication of the language takes places as a separate proceeding and must be concluded *before* the main complaint is filed.[121]

121 ADR Rules, paragraph A3

Complainants must submit to the jurisdiction of the courts in at least one mutual jurisdiction. This is defined[122] as either the respondent's address or the location of the principal office of the registrar. This latter option is only available if the court would be located within the European Union and the respondent submitted to that court's jurisdiction at the time the domain was registered.

In the case of ADR Proceedings against EUR*id* itself, the location of its principal office can also be chosen as a mutual jurisdiction.

Potential complainants should be alive to the risks posed by the mutual jurisdiction clause and the considerations discussed above in the context of the UDRP apply here by analogy.

10.1 The Providers and their differences

The CAC and WIPO are the only two providers of EUR*id* ADR dispute resolution services.

The CAC has been a provider since 2006 and it issued 32 decisions in 2018. It has issued around 1,264 decisions in total. WIPO launched its service on 1 June 2017 and it issued 28 decisions in 2018. These figures generate an estimated dispute rate for 2018 of roughly 0.0017%.

The estimated dispute rate is lower than the equivalent estimates for both the UDRP and the Nominet DRS. This may be due to the fact that the eligibility requirements for *.eu* exclude registrants from the two most common UDRP respondent countries (i.e. the USA and China).

In 2018, 78% of ADR complaints at the CAC resulted in transfer versus 96% of cases filed at WIPO. This gives a combined transfer rate of 87% which is equivalent to that under the UDRP (for single panellist decisions).

122 ADR Rules, paragraph A1

WIPO's transfer rate is noticeably higher but it has not yet been offering these ADR services long enough to determine if it will continue to be at such a high level year-on-year or if this is a statistical blip.

A review of the 2018 decisions shows that there was a higher proportion of clear cybersquatting cases decided against domains that have been registered for some years.[123] It may be, therefore, that complainants had a backlog of cases that they had not brought to the CAC for resolution (perhaps due to unfamiliarity with its procedures).

One further possible explanation for the high transfer rate in the early stages of WIPO's tenure as a provider is that panellists have not yet built up a body of jurisprudence exclusively around the Regulation and the ADR Rules.

Given that panellists at WIPO are very familiar with the UDRP and given the similarities between the ADR Rules and the UDRP, it is perhaps unsurprising that they have been quick to hold that cases decided under both the ADR Rules and the UDRP are relevant.[124] Many panellists are applying UDRP jurisprudence to the less restrictive ADR test and this may have influenced the transfer rate.

As is the position under the UDRP, CAC's panellists are appointed on a cab rank system whereas WIPO specifically chooses and appoints its panellists based on the circumstances of the case.

123 See by way of example *WIPO ADR Case No. DEU2018-0021 <instagram.eu>* and *WIPO ADR Case No. DEU2018-0009 <airbnb.eu>*

124 See by way of example *WIPO ADR Case No. DEU2018-0025 <shoppstyle.eu>* and *WIPO ADR Case No. DEU2018-0004 <crystal-lagoons.eu>*

<u>CAC and WIPO fees</u>

The CAC and WIPO have arranged for EUR*id* to subsidise their fees by EUR 1,200.

This subsidy is a temporary arrangement and it could, therefore, change at short notice, though the CAC and WIPO have stated that the subsidy will continue at least throughout 2025.

The CAC's fee schedule is below:

Number of Domains	Single Panellist Fee (EUR)	Three Panellists Fee (EUR)
1-5	100* [Panellist: 900; CAC: 400]	1,900* [Presiding Panellist: 1,200; Co-Panellists: 600; CAC: 700]
6–10	400* [Panellist: 1,100; CAC: 500]	2,800* [Presiding Panellist: 1,500; Co-Panellists: 800; CAC: 900]
11–20	700* [Panellist: 1,300; CAC: 600]	3,500* [Presiding Panellist: 1,800; Co-Panellists: 900; CAC: 1,100]
21–30	1,000* [Panellist: 1,500; CAC: 700]	4,300* [Presiding Panellist: 2,100; Co-Panellists: 1,050; CAC: 1,300]
31–40	1,300* [Panellist: 1,700; CAC: 800]	5,100* [Presiding Panellist: 2,400; Co-Panellists: 1,200; CAC: 1,500]

41–50	1,600* [Panellist: 1,900; CAC: 900]	5,900* [Presiding Panellist: 2,400; Co-Panellists: 1,200; CAC: 1,700]
≥ 51	To be agreed with CAC on a case-by-case basis	

*includes EUR 1,200 discount

WIPO's fee schedule is below:

Number of Domains	Single Panellist Fee (EUR)	Three Panellists Fee (EUR)
1-5	100* [Panellist: 900; WIPO: 400]	1,900* [Presiding Panellist: 1,200; Co-Panellists: 600; WIPO: 700]
6-10	400* [Panellist: 1,100; WIPO: 500]	2,800* [Presiding Panellist: 1,500; Co-Panellists: 800; WIPO: 900]
> 10	To be agreed with WIPO on a case-by-case basis	

*includes EUR 1,200 discount

These figures are flat rates and no additional fees are payable if panellists call for additional evidence on certain points.

The CAC and WIPO will refund a proportion of the filing fee equivalent to the panellist's fee if settlement occurs before a panel is appointed.

If a complainant submits a request to change the language of the ADR proceeding then this must be accompanied by a fee of EUR 500 [Panellist: EUR 250; WIPO: EUR 250].

If a complainant challenges withdrawal of its complaint (i.e. after a decision that it is deficient on formalities grounds) then this must be accompanied by a fee of EUR 500 [Panellist: EUR 250; WIPO: EUR 250].

10.2 Contents of the complaint and the response

The CAC publishes and maintains an overview of panellist decisions[125] on the ADR requirements and other key questions as well as example complaint forms and response forms.[126] These should without a doubt be the starting points for any party filing a complaint or a response. WIPO has not produced its own competing version of the decision overview.

Panellists are not strictly bound by previous decisions but will treat them as persuasive authority. Accordingly, the most convincing arguments will be based on the consensus views expressed in the CAC.EU Overview document. References to the WIPO Jurisprudential Overview 3.0 may also be relevant if using WIPO as provider.

10.3 The first element

The first element of the test is set out in paragraph B(11)(d)(1)(i) of the ADR Rules. It states (emphasis added):

---

125 CAC.EU Overview 2.0 https://eu.adr.eu/data/handbook-final-second-edidion-2016.pdf

126 https://eu.adr.eu/website/forms

> *(i) The domain name is identical or confusingly similar to a name in respect of which a right is recognized or established by the national law of a Member State and/or European Union law and; either*

The first element test is regarded as a test of standing and, accordingly, the threshold here is a low one.[127] The reference to "confusing" similarity does not import any questions as to whether the use of the domain amounts to trade mark infringement.

Although the first element test has been understood to be a test of the complainant's standing, nowhere in the test does it stipulate that the rights relied upon should in fact be owned by the complainant. On a strict reading of the ADR Rules, therefore, a small minority of panellists had been willing to find that an ADR case can proceed to assessment of the second and third elements even where the complainant does not own the rights on which it relies.

The CAC .EU Overview 2.0 now states[128] that "the complainant in an ADR procedure …has to (inter alia) show that he has rights ..." (emphasis added) and this reflects the majority view.

10.3.1 What types of rights can be relied upon?

The rights are not limited to trade mark rights and any right in a name will suffice provided that the right is recognised or established by EU law or the law of an EU member state.

Examples of non-trade mark rights that are specifically protected under the ADR Rules are geographical indications, designations of origin, trade names, business identifiers, company names, family names and distinctive titles of protected literary and artistic works – provided that

127 See by way of example, *CAC ADR Case No. 05578 <noonan.eu>*

128 Introduction to section II. Relevant rights of the complainant

they are protected under the national law in the member state in which those rights are held.[129]

A right which post-dates the registration of the domain is perfectly acceptable for the purposes of the first element test but, as with the UDRP, the date of creation of the rights will be relevant to the assessments under the second and third elements.

Panellists have not yet reached a firm consensus about whether trade marks registered only outside of the EU are "rights recognised by national and/or European Union law" and thus sufficient to meet the first element test. The majority view is that such rights do give a complainant appropriate standing[130] and this would appear to be a sensible decision. To hold otherwise would be inconsistent with the UDRP and would render the *.eu* ccTLD a haven for cybersquatters.

From first principles, a complainant could argue that it is perfectly normal for a US trade mark applicant to claim Paris Convention priority in the EU from a filing initially made in the USA and that is a clear example of a trade mark right from outside the EU being "recognised" by European Union law.

10.3.2 Identical or confusingly similar

This is a low threshold test and panellists would usually have no difficulty in finding that the domain is identical or confusingly similar if the right is identifiable in the domain name, contains generic additional matter or if it is an obvious typosquatting or spoofing attempt.

As with the UDRP however, some panels have grappled with the idea that the requirement for "confusing" similarity can lead to a complainant falling at the first hurdle where the additional matter is such that no Internet user would be confused into thinking that the domain was

129 ADR Rules paragraph B(1)(9)

130 See by way of example *CAC ADR Case No. 1580 <auntminnie.eu>*

operated by the complainant. This most commonly occurs in cases of fansites, gripesites or unauthorised resellers.

All such cases are to be assessed on the particular circumstances of the case but, in general, panellists prefer to find that confusing similarity under the first element test is present and then decide the dispute under the second and third elements.[131]

10.4 The second element

The second element of the test is set out in paragraph B(11)(d)(1)(ii) of the ADR Rules. It states (emphasis added):

> *(ii) The domain name has been registered by the Respondent* ***without rights or legitimate interest in the name****; or*

The ADR Rules set out at paragraph B11(e) a non-exhaustive list of factors which can support a respondent's claim to legitimate interest in a disputed domain. These include evidence that:

1. Before being made aware of the dispute, the respondent has used (or made demonstrable preparations to use) the domain name in connection with the offering of goods or services

2. The respondent has been commonly known by the domain name

3. The respondent is making a legitimate and non-commercial or fair use of the domain name, without intent to mislead consumers or harm the reputation in the right

These factors will be familiar to UDRP complainants and ADR panellists have approached the issue of legitimate interest similarly to UDRP panellists. The key point of difference under the second element is that if a complainant makes out a *prima facie* case that the respondent has no rights or legitimate interests in the domain name then it can succeed in

131 See by way of example *CAC ADR Case No. 4141 <airfrancesucks.eu>*

its case without the panellist having to go on to consider bad faith under the third element.

10.5 The third element

The third element of the test is set out in paragraph B(11)(d)(1)(iii) of the ADR Rules. It states (emphasis added):

> *(iii) The domain name has been registered **or** is being used in bad faith.*

The first point of note here is that there is no conjunctive requirement and the complaint will succeed if the respondent is shown to have registered the domain in bad faith or subsequently used it in bad faith.

This is a less strict test that the third element of the UDRP but it is more restrictive than the concept of Abusive Registration under the Nominet DRS as the bad faith use must be on-going at the time the complaint is filed.

The ADR Rules set out at paragraph B11(f) a non-exhaustive list of factors which can support a complainant's claim that registration or use of a domain name was in bad faith. These include evidence that:

1. The domain name was registered primarily for the purpose of selling, renting, or otherwise transferring the domain name to the rights holder
2. The domain name has been registered in order to prevent the rights holder from reflecting this name in a corresponding domain name, provided that:
    - (i) the respondent has engaged in a pattern of such conduct; or
    - (ii) the domain name has not been used in a relevant way for at least two years from the date of registration; or

(iii) the respondent has declared its intention to use the domain name but failed to do so within six months of the day on which the ADR Proceeding was initiated

3. The domain name was registered primarily for the purpose of disrupting the professional activities of a competitor; or

4. The domain name was intentionally used to attract traffic for commercial gain by creating a likelihood of confusion; or

5. The domain name is a personal name for which no demonstrable link exists between the respondent and the domain name registered

The final point on this list is the only one that is significantly different to the position under the UDRP where rights in a personal name *per se* are not recognised.

The various other considerations as to bad faith registration and use discussed in the context of the UDRP apply here by analogy.

10.6 Reverse Domain Name Hijacking

Paragraph 12(h) of the ADR Rules allows for a panel to find that a complaint was initiated in bad faith and that it amounted to an abuse of administrative proceeding.

The ADR Rules do not refer to the practice as RDNH and neither does it provide a definition or elaborate on what activities may give rise to such a finding. The matter is left entirely to the discretion of panellists.

The jurisprudence in this area is underdeveloped and panellists seeking to assess RDNH under the ADR Rules will likely be guided by the equivalent principles developed under the UDRP.

There is no set penalty under r the ADR Rules for complainants found guilty of RDNH but such a finding can generate adverse publicity and may prompt the successful respondent to commence related proceedings in a court of mutual jurisdiction.

10.7 Conclusion

The EUR*id* ADR is an underdeveloped system due to the relatively small number of domains registered in the ccTLD and the corresponding lack of ADR cases that come through to adjudication.

The fact that it derives in large part from the UDRP has helped to generate confidence and understanding of the system for potential complainants and their representatives.

If potential complainants are aware of domains that might be the subject of a future complaint then they should file the complaint before the end of 2025 and whilst the subsidy is still in place.

MORE BOOKS BY LAW BRIEF PUBLISHING

A selection of our other titles available now:-

'A Practical Guide to Probation Breaches and Other Applications' by Mark Thomas
'A Practical Guide to Remarriage and Divorce' by Cordelia Williams & Claire Howard
'A Practical Guide to Privacy, Transparency, Reporting Restrictions and Closed Proceedings in the Court of Protection' by Laura Mannering
'Beaumont on Barristers – A Guide to Defending Disciplinary Proceedings (Second Edition)' by Marc Beaumont
'A Practical Guide to Payments for Environmental Services' by Ben Sharples
'A Practical Guide to the Law of Pregnancy and Maternity at Work' by Rebecca Thomas
'A Practical Guide to Redundancy – Second Edition' by Philip Hyland & Collette Moore
'A Practical Guide to International Issues for Scottish Family Lawyers' by Susie Mountain, Donna McKay, Ken MacDonald
'A Practical Guide to the Law on Deprivation of Liberty' by Ben Troke
'A Practical Guide to Rights over Airspace and Subsoil – Second Edition' by Daniel Gatty
'A Practical Guide to the Law in Relation to Inquests' by Ramya Nagesh
'A Practical Guide to the Construction and Rectification of Wills and Trust Instruments (Second Edition)' by Edward Hewitt
'A Practical Guide to Data Protection in Social Housing' by Clare Paterson
'A Practical Guide to Spousal Maintenance – Second Edition' by Liz Cowell
'A Practical Guide to International Parental Child Abduction Law (England and Wales)' by Dr Onyója Momoh
'A Practical Guide to Deprivation of British Citizenship' by Sean Ell
'A Practical Guide to Commercial Property Service Charges' by Rachel Garton
'A Practical Guide to Clinical Negligence – Third Edition' by Geoffrey Simpson-Scott (Geoff)
'A Practical Guide to the Rights of Grandparents in Children Proceedings – Second Edition' by Stuart Barlow

‘The Electronic Communications Code: A Practical Guide – Second Edition’ by Kerry Bretherton KC, James Castle, Mark Loveday

‘A Practical Guide to the Independent School Standards – September 2023 Edition’ by Sarah McKimm

'A Practical Guide to Estate Administration and Crypto Assets' by Richard Marshall

‘A Practical Guide to Parental Alienation in Private and Public Law Children Cases’ by Sam King QC & Frankie Shama

‘Contested Heritage – Removing Art from Land and Historic Buildings’ by Richard Harwood QC, Catherine Dobson, David Sawtell

‘The Limits of Separate Legal Personality: When Those Running a Company Can Be Held Personally Liable for Losses Caused to Third Parties Outside of the Company’ by Dr Mike Wilkinson

‘A Practical Guide to Transgender Law’ by Robin Moira White & Nicola Newbegin

‘A Practical Guide to ‘Stranded Spouses’ in Family Law’ by Mani Singh Basi

‘A Practical Guide to Residential Freehold Conveyancing’ by Lorraine Richardson

‘A Practical Guide to Pensions on Divorce for Lawyers’ by Bryan Scant

‘A Practical Guide to Challenging Sham Marriage Allegations in Immigration Law’ by Priya Solanki

‘A Practical Guide to Digital Communications Evidence in Criminal Law’ by Sam Willis

‘A Practical Guide to Legal Rights in Scotland’ by Sarah-Jane Macdonald

‘A Practical Guide to New Build Conveyancing’ by Paul Sams & Rebecca East

‘A Practical Guide to Inherited Wealth on Divorce’ by Hayley Trim

‘A Practical Guide to Practice Direction 12J and Domestic Abuse in Private Law Children Proceedings’ by Rebecca Cross & Malvika Jaganmohan

‘A Practical Guide to Confiscation and Restraint’ by Narita Bahra QC, John Carl Townsend, David Winch

‘A Practical Guide to the Law of Forests in Scotland’ by Philip Buchan

‘A Practical Guide to Health and Medical Cases in Immigration Law’ by Rebecca Chapman & Miranda Butler

‘A Practical Guide to Bad Character Evidence for Criminal Practitioners by Aparna Rao

‘A Practical Guide to Extradition Law post-Brexit’ by Myles Grandison et al

‘A Practical Guide to Hoarding and Mental Health for Housing Lawyers’ by Rachel Coyle

'Stephens on Contractual Indemnities' by Richard Stephens
'A Practical Guide to the EU Succession Regulation' by Richard Frimston
'A Practical Guide to Solicitor and Client Costs – Second Edition' by Robin Dunne
'Constructive Dismissal – Practice Pointers and Principles' by Benjimin Burgher
'A Practical Guide to Religion and Belief Discrimination Claims in the Workplace' by Kashif Ali
'A Practical Guide to the Law of Medical Treatment Decisions' by Ben Troke
'Fundamental Dishonesty and QOCS in Personal Injury Proceedings: Law and Practice' by Jake Rowley
'A Practical Guide to the Law in Relation to School Exclusions' by Charlotte Hadfield & Alice de Coverley
'A Practical Guide to Divorce for the Silver Separators' by Karin Walker
'The Right to be Forgotten – The Law and Practical Issues' by Melissa Stock
'A Practical Guide to Planning Law and Rights of Way in National Parks, the Broads and AONBs' by James Maurici QC, James Neill et al
'A Practical Guide to Election Law' by Tom Tabori
'A Practical Guide to the Law in Relation to Surrogacy' by Andrew Powell
'A Practical Guide to Claims Arising from Fatal Accidents – Second Edition' by James Patience
'A Practical Guide to Asbestos Claims' by Jonathan Owen & Gareth McAloon
'A Practical Guide to Stamp Duty Land Tax in England and Northern Ireland' by Suzanne O'Hara
'A Practical Guide to the Law of Farming Partnerships' by Philip Whitcomb
'A Practical Guide to the Law of Unlawful Eviction and Harassment – Second Edition' by Stephanie Lovegrove
'A Practical Guide to Costs in Personal Injury Claims – Second Edition' by Matthew Hoe
'A Practical Guide to the General Data Protection Regulation (GDPR) – Second Edition' by Keith Markham
'A Practical Guide to Working with Litigants in Person and McKenzie Friends in Family Cases' by Stuart Barlow
'Protecting Unregistered Brands: A Practical Guide to the Law of Passing Off' by Lorna Brazell
'A Practical Guide to Secondary Liability and Joint Enterprise Post-Jogee' by Joanne Cecil & James Mehigan

'A Practical Guide to the Pre-Action RTA Claims Protocol for Personal Injury Lawyers' by Antonia Ford

'A Practical Guide to Neighbour Disputes and the Law' by Alexander Walsh

'A Practical Guide to Coercive Control for Legal Practitioners and Victims' by Rachel Horman

'A Practical Guide to the Law of Driverless Cars – Second Edition'

by Alex Glassbrook, Emma Northey & Scarlett Milligan

'A Practical Guide to TOLATA Claims' by Greg Williams

'A Practical Guide to Elderly Law – Second Edition' by Justin Patten

'A Practical Guide to Responding to Housing Disrepair and Unfitness Claims' by Iain Wightwick

'A Practical Guide to the Law of Bullying and Harassment in the Workplace' by Philip Hyland

'How to Be a Freelance Solicitor: A Practical Guide to the SRA-Regulated Freelance Solicitor Model' by Paul Bennett

'A Practical Guide to Prison Injury Claims' by Malcolm Johnson

'A Practical Guide to Advising Clients at the Police Station' by Colin Stephen McKeown-Beaumont

'A Practical Guide to Antisocial Behaviour Injunctions – Second Edition' by Iain Wightwick

'Practical Mediation: A Guide for Mediators, Advocates, Advisers, Lawyers, and Students in Civil, Commercial, Business, Property, Workplace, and Employment Cases' by Jonathan Dingle with John Sephton

'The Mini-Pupillage Workbook' by David Boyle

'A Practical Guide to Crofting Law' by Brian Inkster

'A Practical Guide to the Law of Domain Names and Cybersquatting' by Andrew Clemson

'A Practical Guide to the Law of Gender Pay Gap Reporting' by Harini Iyengar

'NHS Whistleblowing and the Law' by Joseph England

'Employment Law and the Gig Economy' by Nigel Mackay & Annie Powell

'A Practical Guide to Noise Induced Hearing Loss (NIHL) Claims' by Andrew Mckie, Ian Skeate, Gareth McAloon

'An Introduction to Beauty Negligence Claims – A Practical Guide for the Personal Injury Practitioner' by Greg Almond

'Intercompany Agreements for Transfer Pricing Compliance' by Paul Sutton

'Zen and the Art of Mediation' by Martin Plowman

'A Practical Guide to Adoption for Family Lawyers' by Graham Pegg

- ‘A Practical Guide to Industrial Disease Claims’ by Andrew Mckie & Ian Skeate
- ‘A Practical Guide to Conducting a Sheriff Court Proof’ by Andrew Stevenson
- ‘A Practical Guide to Vicarious Liability’ by Mariel Irvine
- ‘A Practical Guide to Applications for Landlord’s Consent and Variation of Leases’ by Mark Shelton
- ‘A Practical Guide to Relief from Sanctions Post-Mitchell and Denton’ by Peter Causton
- ‘A Practical Guide to Equity Release for Advisors’ by Paul Sams
- ‘A Practical Guide to Financial Services Claims’ by Chris Hegarty
- ‘A Practical Guide to Financial Ombudsman Service Claims’ by Adam Temple & Robert Scrivenor
- ‘A Practical Guide to Running Housing Disrepair and Cavity Wall Claims – Second Edition’ by Andrew Mckie & Ian Skeate
- ‘A Practical Guide to Holiday Sickness Claims – Second Edition’ by Andrew Mckie & Ian Skeate
- ‘Arguments and Tactics for Personal Injury and Clinical Negligence Claims’ by Dorian Williams
- ‘A Practical Guide to Drone Law’ by Rufus Ballaster, Andrew Firman, Eleanor Clot
- ‘On Experts: CPR35 for Lawyers and Experts’ by David Boyle
- ‘An Introduction to Personal Injury Law’ by David Boyle

These books and more are available to order online direct from the publisher at www.lawbriefpublishing.com, where you can also read free sample chapters. For any queries, call us on 0844 587 2383 or email us at mail@lawbriefpublishing.com.

Our books are all generally in stock at www.amazon.co.uk with free next day delivery for Prime members, and at good legal bookshops such as Wildy & Sons.

We are regularly launching new books in our series of practical day-to-day practitioners' guides. Visit our website and join our free newsletter to be kept informed and to receive special offers, free chapters, etc.

You can also follow us on Twitter at www.twitter.com/lawbriefpub.

www.ingramcontent.com/pod-product-compliance
Lightning Source LLC
LaVergne TN
LVHW022045200926
848481LV00003B/797

9781918241082